STREET SPANISH

*How to Speak and Understand
Spanish Slang*

David Burke

John Wiley & Sons, Inc.
New York • Chichester • Brisbane • Toronto • Singapore

Publisher: David Sobel
Editor: Steve Ross
Managing Editor: Ruth Greif
Editing, Design, and Production: Optima PrePress
Cover Illustration: Paul Jermann
Inside Illustrations: Shawn Murphy

This publication is designed to provide accurate and authoritative information in regard to the subject matter covered. It is sold with the understanding that the publisher is not engaged in rendering legal, accounting, or other professional services. If legal advice or other expert assistance is required, the services of a competent professional person should be sought. FROM A DECLARATION OF PRINCIPLES JOINTLY ADOPTED BY A COMMITTEE OF THE AMERICAN BAR ASSOCIATION AND A COMMITTEE OF PUBLISHERS.

Recognizing the importance of preserving what has been written, it is a policy of John Wiley & Sons, Inc. to have books of enduring value published in the United States printed on acid-free paper, and we exert our best efforts to that end.

Library of Congress Cataloging-in-Publication Data
Burke, David, 1956-
    Street Spanish : how to speak and understand Spanish slang /
David Burke.
    p.   cm.
ISBN 0-471-52846-3
    1. Spanish language – Slang. 2. Spanish language – Slang –
–Glossaries, vocabularies, etc. I. Title.
PC3739.B86   1989
447'.09 – dc20   90-43297
                                                  CIP

Printed in the United States of America
91 92 10 9 8 7 6 5 4 3 2 1

THIS BOOK IS DEDICATED TO MOM, TOM, NANCY & DOM

PREFACE

STREET SPANISH presents a step-by-step approach to the teaching of common idiomatic expressions and slang that constantly appear in movies, books, and day-to-day business transactions, as well as among family and friends. The book is destined to open new doors quickly as you enter the "secret" world of slang and learn the "inside" language that even a ten-year veteran of formal Spanish training would not understand!

STREET SPANISH will lead you through the colorful world of idiomatic expressions in fifteen lessons. Each lesson is divided into three parts:

1. **DIALOGUE**: Here you will encounter twenty to thirty new Spanish expressions, indicated in boldface, that are used in context to demonstrate correct usage. An English translation of the dialogue is always given on the opposite page followed by a *literal* translation which often proves to be hilarious.

2. **VOCABULARY**: This section gives a detailed explanation of each slang term or expression used in the dialogue, along with its synonym and/or antonym. Pay careful attention to these expressions because they may appear again in one of the subsequent dialogues! In addition, a literal translation will be offered whenever possible.

   In this section, you may also encounter two special entries found under a particular term or expression:

   NOTE: Here you will be given specific notes regarding origin, common variations, and any other pertinent details.

   ALSO: This segment demonstrates other ways in which the main word from the vocabulary can be used in other expressions as well.

3. **PRACTICE THE VOCABULARY**: These drills and word games will allow you to test yourself on the expressions from the dialogue. Feel free to write directly on the page as this is also your workbook. (The pages providing the answers to all the drills are indicated at the beginning of this section.)

   Following each sequence of five chapters is a review exam encompassing all of the words and expressions learned up to that point.

Also, unique to this book is a detailed list of common mistakes made by unsuspecting foreigners who learn Spanish used in one country then use these expressions in another country and find themselves reeling off obscenities unknowingly!

The secret to learning **STREET SPANISH** is to follow this simple checklist:

- Make sure that you have a good grasp of each section before proceeding to the drills. If you've made more than two errors in a particular drill, simply go back and review– then try again. Remember: This is a self-paced book, so take your time. You're not fighting the clock!

- It's very important that you feel comfortable with each chapter before proceeding to the next since words learned along the way may be used again in the following lessons. So feel comfortable before moving on!

- Read the dialogues and drills aloud. This is an excellent way to help you speak colloquially and think like a native!

Just as a student of formal English would be rather shocked to run into expressions like *to freak out, to be ticked off,* and *to be pooped,* you too will be surprised and amused to encounter a whole new array of phrases usually hidden away in the Spanish language and reserved only for the native speaker.

Welcome to the expressive and colorful world of slang!

David Burke

LEGEND

adj.	adjective	(lit)	literal translation
adv.	adverb	m.	masculine
exclam.	exclamation	n.	noun
exp.	expression	pl.	plural
f.	feminine	Prn.	proper name
interj.	interjection	v.	verb

ACKNOWLEDGMENTS

Once again, I cannot thank my family and friends enough for being so tolerant every time I would stop the conversation, pull out my note pad and say, "*Oh, that's a great expression! Let me write that down!*" It was their inspiration that has propelled me into writing my third book on slang.

I am very grateful to Miguel Alvarez, Ana Laura Faro and Teresa Chimienti for making the copy editing phase of the book such a pleasure. Their dedication, precision, and resolve was very impressive and will always be tremendously appreciated.

I owe a great deal of gratitude to Katherine Schowalter whose encouragement and support gave me the enthusiasm to continue to explore the diverse use of slang in other countries; to Steve Ross who, due to his passion and excitement for the Spanish language, was the driving force behind this book; and to John Wiley & Sons for allowing me to work with a production manager and friend of the highest caliber, Ruth Greif who, as usual, made the entire production process an absolute delight.

CONTENTS

UNIT TWO
Being Obscene Unintentionally   199
(and other embarrassing moments)

GLOSSARY   207

LESSON ONE

En la escuela

(At School)

¡No la puedo ver ni en pintura! Entre paréntesis, creo que le falta un tornillo.

¡Le diste en el clavo!

EN LA ESCUELA...

DIÁLOGO

Ana está **chismeando** con Inés.

Ana:	**¿Qué hay de nuevo?**
Inés:	Déjame contarte, **tropecé** con María en la calle y me detuve a **platicar** con ella. Pero sabes es **muy ligera de palabra**. ¡Habla **como loca** y a veces **no entiendo ni papa**! Siempre **se ahoga en un vaso de agua**.
Ana:	**¡No la puedo ver ni en pintura!** Todos sus cuentos son **traídos por los pelos**. **Entre paréntesis**, creo que **le falta un tornillo**.
Inés:	**¡Le diste en el clavo!**
Ana:	A ver, **ponme al día**.
Inés:	María **está en un apuro**. El profesor **le dio calabazas** por **hacer la pinta**.
Ana:	**¡Me estás tomando el pelo!**
Inés:	**¡Nones!**
Ana:	**¡Perdí el habla!** Esta vez creo que **se pasó de raya**. Siempre **le busca tres pies al gato**. Supongo que el profesor está **hasta la coronilla de** ella.
Inés:	Uno de estos días, la voy a **mandar a freír espárragos**.
Ana:	**¿Para qué? Le entra por un oído y le sale por el otro.** Gastarías **saliva en balde**. ¿Estaba enojada su mamá?
Inés:	**¡Puso el grito en el cielo!** María me dijo que **la puso como un trapo**.
Ana:	Y su madre **tiene malas pulgas** todo el tiempo.
Inés:	Ella es de verdad **la oveja negra de la familia**.

Lesson One

AT SCHOOL...

DIALOGUE

Ana is gossiping with Inés.

Ana: What's new?

Inés: Let me tell you, I ran into Maria in the street and stopped to have a little chat with her. But you know what a blabbermouth she is. She goes on and on and sometimes I don't understand a thing! She always seems upset about something.

Ana: I can't stand her! All her stories are so farfetched. By the way, I think she's not playing with a full deck.

Inés: You got that one right!

Ana: Give me the lowdown.

Inés: Maria got herself into a real mess. The teacher flunked her for cutting class.

Ana: You're pulling my leg!

Inés: Nope!

Ana: I'm speechless! This time I think she went too far. She's always looking for trouble. I suppose the teacher just had it up to here with her.

Inés: One of these days, I'm going to tell her off.

Ana: What for? It just goes in one ear and out the other. You'd be wasting your breath. Was her mother mad?

Inés: She hit the ceiling! Maria told me that she really raked her over the coals.

Ana: And her mother is short-tempered all the time.

Inés: She really is the black sheep of the family.

Literal Translation of Dialogue

DIALOGUE

Ana is telling Inés some gossip.

Ana:	What's new?
Inés:	Let me tell you, I tripped with Maria in the street and stopped to have a chat with her. But you know she's very light with words. She talks like a crazy woman and sometimes I don't understand a potato! She always drowns in a glass of water.
Ana:	I can't even look at a painting of her! All her stories are carried by the hairs. In parenthesis, I think she's missing a screw.
Inés:	You gave it in the nail!
Ana:	To see, bring me to the day.
Inés:	Maria is in a real fix. The professor gave her pumpkins for making the stain.
Ana:	You're taking my hair!
Inés:	Nope!
Ana:	I've lost my speech! This time I think she's crossed the line. She's always looking for three of the cat's feet. I suppose the teacher had it up to the crown of his head with her.
Inés:	One of these days, I'm going to tell her to go fry asparagus.
Ana:	For what? It goes in one ear and out the other. You'd be wasting your saliva in a bucket. Was her mother mad?
Inés:	Her mother put the scream to the sky! Maria told me that she put her like a rag.
Ana:	And her mother has bad fleas all the time.
Inés:	She really is the black sheep of the family.

VOCABULARY

ahogarse en un vaso de agua *exp.* to get all worked up about nothing, to make a mountain out of a molehill • (lit); to drown in a glass of water.
    SYNONYM: **ahogarse en poca agua** *exp.* • (lit); to drown in a little water.
    ALSO: **ahogar en germen** *exp.* to nip in the bud • (lit); to drown while it's still only a germ.

buscarle tres pies al gato *exp.* to go looking for trouble • (lit); to look for three of the cat's feet.
    SYNONYM (1): **buscarle cinco pies al gato** *exp.* • (lit); to look for five of the cat's feet.
    SYNONYM (2): **buscarle mangas al chaleco** *exp.* • (lit); to look for sleeves in the vest.
    NOTE (1): **buscarle los tres pies al gato** *exp.* (Cuba) Note that in Cuba, the definite article *los* is used before *tres pies.*
    NOTE (2): **buscarle cinco pies al gato** *exp.* (Ecuador) to go looking for trouble • (lit); to search for a five-footed cat.

chismear *v.* to gossip
    NOTE: **chisme** *m.* a juicy piece of gossip • *¡Cuéntame los chismes!;* Give me the dirt!
    SYNONYM: **chispazo** *m.* • (lit); spark.
    ALSO: **chismorrear** *v.* to gossip, to blab (a variant of *chismear*).

dar calabazas a uno *exp.* **1.** to fail someone • **2.** to jilt someone • (lit); to give someone pumpkins.
    NOTE (1): **recibir calabazas** *exp.* **1.** to fail (a test) • **2.** to get jilted • (lit); to receive pumpkins.
    NOTE (2): Interestingly enough, an amusing variation of the expression *dar calabazas* has been created in which the feminine noun *calabaza* meaning "pumpkin" has been transformed into the slang verb *calabacear* meaning "to fail (someone) or to jilt" or literally, "to pumpkin (someone)."

dar en el clavo *exp.* to hit the nail on the head, to put one's finger on it • (lit); to hit on the nail.
    ALSO: **ser capaz de clavar un clavo con la cabeza** *exp.* to be pigheaded, stubborn • (lit); to be capable of hammering a nail with the head.
    SYNONYM: **dar en el hito** *exp.* • (lit); to hit on the stone.
    NOTE: **dar en** *exp.* to hit on • (lit); to give on.

entrar por un oído y salir por el otro *exp.* to go in one ear and out the other.
    ALSO: **ser todos oídos** *exp.* to be all ears.

entre paréntesis *exp.* by the way, incidentally • (lit); in parentheses.

estar en un apuro *m.* to be in a difficult situation, in a jam • (lit); to be in a difficulty.
  ANTONYM: **sacar del apuro** *exp.* to get out of a jam • (lit); to get out of a difficulty.

estar (uno) hasta la coronilla de *exp.* to be fed up with, to have had it up to here with • (lit); to be up to the crown of one's head with.
  SYNONYM: **estar hasta la punta del pelo (de)** *exp.* • (lit); to be up to the ends of the hair with • ALSO: **estar hasta los pelos (de)** *exp.* • (lit); to be up to the hairs with.

faltar un tornillo *exp.* to be crazy, to have a screw loose • (lit); to miss a screw • *Le falta un tornillo*; He's/She's missing a screw.
  SYNONYM (1): **tener flojos los tornillos** *exp.* • (lit); to have loose screws.
  SYNONYM (2): **estar chiflado(a)** *exp.* • (lit); to be crazy, cracked.
  SYNONYM (3): **tener los alambres pelados** *exp.* (Chile) • (lit); to have smooth bells.

gastar saliva en balde *exp.* to waste one's breath (while explaining something to someone) • **1. gastar saliva** *exp.* to waste one's breath • (lit); to waste one's saliva • **2. en balde** *exp.* for nothing, in vain • (lit); in a pail, bucket.
  ALSO: **de balde** *exp.* free of charge.

hablar como loco(a) *exp.* to speak nonstop • (lit); to speak like crazy, like mad.
  NOTE: **como loco(a)** *exp.* like crazy, like mad • *correr como loco;* to run like mad.
  ALSO: **tener una suerte loca** *exp.* to have unbelievable luck • (lit); to have (a) crazy luck.
  SYNONYM (1): **hablar como una cotorra** *exp.* • (lit); to talk like a magpie.
  SYNONYM (2): **no parar la boca** *exp.* (Mexico) • (lit); not to stop (flapping) one's mouth.
  SYNONYM (3): **hablar hasta por los codos** *exp.* • (lit); to talk even with the elbows.
  SYNONYM (4): **ser lengua larga** *exp.* to gossip • (lit); to be long-tongued.

hacer la pinta *exp.* to cut class • (lit); to make the spot.
  NOTE: This is a humorous expression which conjures up an image of someone leaving behind nothing more than a spot or mark as proof that he/she was once there.
  SYNONYM: **fumarse una clase** *exp.* to cut a class • (lit); to smoke a class.

mandar a alguien a freír espárragos *exp.* to tell someone to take a flying leap • (lit); to send someone to fry asparagus.
  SYNONYM: **mandar a alguien a freír monas** *exp.* • (lit); to send someone to fry female monkeys.

no entender ni papa *exp.* not to understand a thing • (lit); not to understand a potato.
ALSO: **no saber ni papa de** *exp.* not to know a thing about, not to have a clue about • (lit); not to know a potato about.
NOTE: **papa** *f.* potato • **papa** *m.* Pope • **papá** *m.* father, daddy.

no poder ver a uno ni en pintura *exp.* not to be able to stand someone • (lit); not to be able to even look at a painting of someone (as just their mere image would be too much to bear).
SYNONYM (1): **no poder con** *exp.* • (lit); not to be able to put up with.
SYNONYM (2): **no ser un hueso fácil de roer** *exp.* not to be easy to tolerate • (lit); not to be an easy bone to gnaw.
SYNONYM (3): **no tragar a alguien** *exp.* not to be able to stomach someone • (lit); not to swallow someone.

nones *adv.* (Mexico) no, nope.
SYNONYM: **nel** *adv.* (Mexico)

¿para qué? *conj.* why? what for? • (lit); for what?

pasarse de raya *exp.* to go too far, to overstep one's bounds • (lit); to cross the line.

perder el habla *exp.* to be speechless • (lit); to lose one's speech.
SYNONYM: **quedarse mudo** *exp.* • (lit); to remain mute.

poner a uno al día *exp.* to bring someone up-to-date • (lit); to put one at the day.
NOTE: **estar al día** *exp.* to be up-to-date.
SYNONYM (1): **poner a uno al corriente** *exp.* • (lit); to put one at the current (moment).
SYNONYM (2): **poner a uno al tanto** *exp.* • (lit); to put one at the point (in a score).

poner a uno como un trapo *exp.* to rake someone over the coals • (lit); to put one like a rag.
SYNONYM: **poner a uno como campeón** *exp.* (Mexico) • (lit); to put one like a champion.

poner el grito en el cielo *exp.* to raise the roof, to scream with rage • (lit); to put a scream in the sky.

¿Qué hay de nuevo? *exp.* • (lit); What's new?
NOTE: **de nuevo** *adv.* again • *Lo hizo de nuevo;* He/She did it again.
SYNONYM: **¿Qué hubo?** *exp.* (Mexico, Colombia) What's up?

ser la oveja negra de la familia *exp.* • (lit); to be the black sheep of the family.

ser muy ligero(a) de palabra *exp.* to be very talkative • (lit); to be very light with words.

tener malas pulgas *exp.* to be irritable, ill-tempered • (lit); to have bad fleas.

tomarle el pelo a uno *exp.* to pull someone's leg • (lit); to take someone's hair. SYNONYM: **hacerle guaje a uno** *exp.* (Mexico) • (lit); to make a fool of someone.

traer por los pelos *exp.* to be farfetched • (lit); to be carried by the hairs • *Me parece un poco traído por los pelos;* I think it's a little farfetched.

tropezarse con alguien *exp.* to run into someone, to bump into someone • (lit); to trip or stumble with someone.

PRACTICE THE VOCABULARY

[Answers to Lesson 1, p. 51]

A. Underline the appropriate word.

1. No te imaginas con quien me (**calabacé, tropecé, traje por los pelos**) en el mercado hoy.

2. No puedo verlo ni en (**fotografía, apuro, pintura**).

3. ¡No entiendo ni (**papa, papá, papel**)!

4. María siempre se ahoga en un (**jarro, tazón, vaso**) de agua.

5. –¿Has visto mi perro? –(**Nones, Nona, Nogal**).

6. ¡Cuéntame los (**pies, chismes, trapos**)!

7. Lucía me cae muy bien pero entre (**paréntesis, parentescos, paridad**), es un poco rara.

8. ¡Pónme al (**noche, día, mes**)! ¿Qué ha pasado últimamente?

9. ¿Qué hay de (**nuevo, chisme, papa**)?

10. Perdí (**el habla, el oído, la vista**) cuando me enteré que Enrique estaba en un (**apunte, apuramiento, apuro**) otra vez.

11. –Voy a ir a comprar una sierra. –¿Para (**que, qué, quebrada**)?

12. Ella es de verdad la (**oveja, ovejera, overa**) negra de la familia.

B. Complete the phrases by choosing the appropriate word(s) from the list below. Make all necessary changes.

ahogarse

calabazas

grito en el cielo

clavo

ligero

oído

buscarle

tomarle

coronilla

espárragos

pasarse

trapo

1. La voy a mandar a freír _____ .

2. Su madre estaba tan enojada que puso el _____ .

3. Es muy _____ de palabra.

4. Me estás _____ el pelo!

5. Le entra por un _____ y le sale por el otro.

6. María me dijo que su mamá la puso como un _____ .

7. Siempre _____ tres pies al gato.

8. El profesor le dio _____ .

9. Esta vez creo que _____ de raya.

10. ¡Le diste en el _____ !

11. El profesor está hasta la _____ de ella.

12. Siempre _____ en un vaso de agua.

C. Circle the words in the grid that fit the expressions below. Words may be spelled in any direction, even backwards or upside down! The first one has been done for you.

1. _____ *m.* a juicy piece of gossip.
2. **estar en un** _____ *exp.* to be in a difficult situation, in a jam.
3. **entre** _____ *exp.* by the way, incidentally.
4. **dar en el** _____ *exp.* to hit the nail on the head.
5. **poner a uno al** _____ *exp.* to bring someone up-to-date.
6. _____ **con** *exp.* to run into someone, to bump into someone.
7. **poner a uno como un** _____ *exp.* to rake someone over the coals.
8. **hacer la** _____ *exp.* to cut class.
9. **gastar saliva en** _____ *exp.* to waste one's breath.
10. **no entender ni** _____ *exp.* not to understand a thing.

O	P	A	R	T	B	P	U	X	E	P	F
D	M	P	A	R	É	N	T	E	S	I	S
E	M	X	É	R	A	P	D	R	J	N	S
S	C	F	F	E	B	U	A	W	T	T	Y
A	L	R	Y	O	E	Z	J	P	K	A	P
D	A	A	V	I	E	D	B	U	A	R	K
T	V	O	N	P	M	Í	É	G	R	A	U
P	O	E	O	G	O	C	H	I	S	M	E
M	Y	R	M	O	R	M	F	I	E	D	D
D	T	E	G	N	U	E	Y	U	L	U	D
N	B	D	F	E	P	E	J	A	E	W	U
Q	É	W	H	B	A	D	B	E	D	Í	A

D. Match the Spanish with the English translations by writing the appropriate letter in the box.

☐ 1. You'd be wasting your breath.

☐ 2. I don't understand a thing.

☐ 3. This time she's gone too far.

☐ 4. Tell me the dirt.

☐ 5. My sister is always in a bad mood.

☐ 6. She's always looking for trouble.

☐ 7. The teacher is fed up with her.

☐ 8. You hit it on the head.

☐ 9. Maria cut class yesterday.

☐ 10. She talks like crazy.

☐ 11. I think she's got a screw loose.

☐ 12. What's new?

A. **¿Qué hay de nuevo?**

B. **Le diste en el clavo.**

C. **Creo que le falta un tornillo.**

D. **No entiendo ni papa.**

E. **Ella siempre le busca tres pies al gato.**

F. **Habla como loca.**

G. **Cuéntame los chismes.**

H. **Gastarías saliva en balde.**

I. **María hizo la pinta ayer.**

J. **El profesor está hasta la coronilla de ella.**

K. **Mi hermana tiene malas pulgas todo el tiempo.**

L. **Esta vez se pasó de raya.**

LESSON TWO

En la fiesta

(At the Party)

¡Dichosos los ojos! Me da gusto que hiciste acto de presencia y como siempre estás de gala.

Gracias.

EN LA FIESTA...

DIÁLOGO

Ricardo y Adriana **están de parranda** y se encuentran.

Ricardo:	**¡Dichosos los ojos!** Me da gusto que **hiciste acto de presencia** y como siempre estás **de gala**.
Adriana:	Gracias.
Ricardo:	¿Qué te parece si nos **echamos un trago? Te convido** a una copa de Kahlúa. **Va por cuenta de la casa.**
Adriana:	Eres una **dulzura**.
Ricardo:	Me lo han dicho **más de cuatro**.
Adriana:	¿Has probado la comida? Se me **hace agua la boca**.
Ricardo:	Ya sé. Está **para chuparse los dedos.** Ana es una cocinera excelente. **Se deshace por** sus amigos. También su esposo. ¿Sabías que sólo tiene treinta **abriles**?
Adriana:	¡No es cierto!
Ricardo:	**Me lo dijo en las barbas.** Está muy bien **conservado**.
Adriana:	**Te tragaste el anzuelo**. Trató de darte **gato por liebre**. Pero **le conozco el juego**. No sé por qué siempre **se quita los años**.
Ricardo:	Siempre he creído que **era buena onda**. Me pregunto por qué lo hace.
Adriana:	**Está tan claro como el agua.** Sabe que siempre será **un cero a la izquierda** y por eso **habla a mil por hora** para que no le hagan demasiadas preguntas. Además, sus respuestas son **puras mentiras**. Y siempre **mete la cuchara**. Cuidado con lo que dices delante de él. Y no es el único aquí que es así. Por eso está **como un pez en el agua** cuando se reúne con esta gente.

Lesson Two

AT THE PARTY...

DIALOGUE

Ricardo and Adriana are out partying and run into each other.

Ricardo: How nice to see you! I'm glad you decided to put in an appearance and as usual you look beautiful!

Adriana: Thank you.

Ricardo: What do you say we have a drink. I'll treat you to a glass of Kahlúa. It's on the house.

Adriana: Aren't you a sweetheart!

Ricardo: Quite a few people have told me that.

Adriana: Have you tried the food? It makes my mouth water.

Ricardo: I know. It's delicious. Ana is an excellent cook. She really puts herself out for her friends. So does her husband. Did you know he's only thirty years old?

Adriana: Impossible!

Ricardo: He told me right to my face. He does look well-preserved.

Adriana: Well, you swallowed that hook, line and sinker. He tried to pull the wool over your eyes. But I'm on to him. I don't know why he always lies about his age.

Ricardo: I always thought he was a nice guy. I wonder why he does that.

Adriana: It's as plain as day. He knows he'll never amount to anything, so he talks a mile a minute so that you don't have a chance to ask him too many questions. Besides, his answers are all lies! And he always butts in. Just be careful what you say in front of him. And he's not the only one here like that! That's why he feels right at home around these people.

Literal Translation of Dialogue

DIALOGUE

Ricardo and Adriana are out partying and meet each other.

Ricardo:	Fortunate the eyes! It gives me pleasure that you made an act of presence and as usual you're in such regalia!
Adriana:	Thank you.
Ricardo:	What do you think if we threw a swallow? I invite you to a glass of Kahlúa. It goes on the account of the house.
Adriana:	You're a sweetness.
Ricardo:	More than four have told me that.
Adriana:	Have you tasted the food? It makes my mouth water.
Ricardo:	I already know. It is to suck one's fingers. Ana is an excellent cook. She undoes herself for her friends. Her husband also. Did you know he only has thirty Aprils?
Adriana:	It isn't true!
Ricardo:	He told me in my beards. He's very well-preserved.
Adriana:	You swallowed the hook. He tried to give you a cat for a hare. But I know his game. I don't know why he always takes away the years.
Ricardo:	I always thought he was a good wave. I ask myself why he does that.
Adriana:	It's as clear as water. He knows he'll always be a zero to the left and that's why he talks a thousand an hour so that people can't ask him too many questions. Besides his answers are pure lies. And he always puts in the spoon. Be careful with what you say in front of him. And he's not the only one like that here. For that, he's like a fish in the water when he gets together with these people.

VOCABULARY

conocerle el juego *exp.* to be on to someone • (lit); to know someone's game.

convidar a *v.* to treat (someone) to (something) • (lit); to invite to • *Me convidó a una copa de Kahlúa;* He/She treated me to a glass of Kahlúa.

dar gato por liebre *exp.* to cheat, deceive, put something over on someone • (lit); to give cat for hare.
  SYNONYM (1): **hacerle guaje a uno** *exp.* (Mexico) • (lit); to make a fool of someone.
  SYNONYM (2): **pasársela a uno** *exp.* (Chile) • (lit); to go too far with someone.

deshacerse por *exp.* to bust one's buns in order to do something, to bend over backwards • (lit); to undo oneself for.

dichosos los ojos *exp.* how nice to see you • (lit); fortunate the eyes.
  ALSO: **costar/valer un ojo de la cara** *exp.* to cost an arm and a leg • (lit); to cost/to be worth an eye of the face.

dulzura *f.* sweetheart • (lit); sweetness.
  NOTE: Other terms of endearment include: *mi alma, mi cielo, mi cariño, amor mío, mi amor, mi pichón, mi corazón, etc.*

echarse un trago *exp.* to have oneself a drink • (lit); to throw a swallow.
  NOTE (1): The verb *tragar,* which literally means "to swallow," is commonly used to mean "to eat voraciously." It is interesting to note that as a noun, *trago* means "a drink." However, when used as a verb, *tragar* takes on the meaning of "to eat": *¿Quieres echar un trago?;* Would you care for a drink? • *¿Qué quieres tragar?;* What would you like to eat?
  SYNONYM (1): **empinar el codo** *exp.* • (lit); to raise the elbow.
  SYNONYM (2): **echarse un fogonazo** *exp.* (Mexico) • (lit); to throw oneself a flash.
  SYNONYM (3): **empinar el cacho** *exp.* (Chile) • (lit); to raise the piece.
  SYNONYM (4): **pegarse un palo** *exp.* (Cuba, Puerto Rico, Dominican Republic, Colombia) • (lit); to stick oneself a gulp.
  SYNONYM (5): **darse un palo** *exp.* (Cuba) • (lit); to give oneself a gulp.
  ALSO: **duro de tragar** *exp.* hard to believe • (lit); hard to swallow.

en las barbas *exp.* in one's face • (lit); in one's beards.
  ALSO: **reírse en las barbas de uno** *exp.* to laugh in one's face • (lit); to laugh in one's beards.

estar bien conservado(a) *exp.* • (lit); to be well-preserved.
   ANTONYM: **estar con piel de pasa** *exp.* to look old • (lit); to be with raisin skin.

estar como un pez en el agua *exp.* to be in one's element, to feel right at home • (lit); to be like a fish in the water.
   ALSO: **pez gordo** *m.* big shot, bigwig • (lit); fat fish.
   NOTE: **pez** is a live fish; **pescado** is a fish that has been prepared as food.

estar de gala *exp.* to be all dressed up, to be in formal attire, to be dressed to kill • (lit); to be in full regalia.

estar de parranda *exp.* to be out partying.
   SYNONYM (1): **andar de parranda** *exp.* to go out partying.
   SYNONYM (2): **parrandear** *v.* to go out partying.
   SYNONYM (3): **irse de juerga** *exp.* to paint the town red • (lit); to go on a binge.
   SYNONYM (4): **irse de tuna** *exp.* (Colombia) to go on a spree, to paint the town red • (lit); to go (running around) for female students.
   SYNONYM (5): **irse de farras** *exp.* (Eastern Argentina, Uruguay) to party it up • (lit); to go for lavarets (a type of fish).
   SYNONYM (6): **irse de jarana** *exp.* (Venezuela) to go partying, to go on a binge • (lit); to go make a rumpus, a lot of noise.
   SYNONYM (7): **irse de rumba** *exp.* (Cuba, Puerto Rico, Dominican Republic) to go partying • (lit); to go for a rumba.
   NOTE (1): **parrandero(a)** *n.* party animal.
   NOTE (2): **parrandeo** *m.* party.
   NOTE (3): **pachanga** *f.* party.

estar tan claro(a) como el agua *exp.* to be crystal clear (i.e. a concept, etc.) • (lit); to be as clear as the water.

hablar a mil por hora *exp.* to talk non-stop • (lit); to talk a thousand (miles) per hour.

hacer acto de presencia *exp.* to put in an appearance • (lit); to make an act of presence.

hacérsele agua la boca *exp.* to make one's mouth water • (lit); to turn one's mouth into water.

más de cuatro *exp.* several people • (lit); more than four (people).

meter la cuchara *exp.* to meddle, to butt in • (lit); to put the spoon in.

para chuparse los dedos *exp.* delicious • (lit); to suck or lick one's fingers.
   NOTE: A popular Spanish advertisement: *Kentucky Fried Chicken está para chuparse los dedos;* Kentucky Fried Chicken is finger lickin' good.

puras mentiras *exp.* pure lies.

NOTE: The adjective *puro* can be used to mean "complete" or "utter" as in the expression *puras papas* meaning "absolutely nothing": *¿Qué te dio para tu cumpleaños? -¡Puras papas!;* -What did he/she give you for your birthday? -Absolutely nothing! • *pura flojera:* pure laziness • (lit); pure looseness.

quitarse los años *exp.* to lie about one's age • (lit); to take off one's years.

ser buena onda *exp.* (Mexico) to be a "good egg" • (lit); to be a good wave.

ser un cero a la izquierda *exp.* said of someone who is a real zero, who will never amount to anything • (lit); to be a zero to the left (of the decimal point).

tener...abriles *exp.* to be...years old • (lit); to have...Aprils.

tragarse el anzuelo *exp.* to swallow something hook, line, and sinker • (lit); to swallow the hook.

va por cuenta de la casa *exp.* it's on the house • (lit); it goes on the account of the house.

PRACTICE THE VOCABULARY

[Answers to Lesson 2, p. 53]

A. Underline the synonym.

1.	**parranda:**	a. fierro	b. fiesta
2.	**más de cuatro:**	a. muchas personas	b. muchísimo
3.	**dulzura:**	a. carro	b. cariño
4.	**estar bien conservado:**	a. parecer viejo	b. parecer joven
5.	**tragarse el anzuelo:**	a. creer una mentira	b. comer mucho
6.	**estar de gala:**	a. estar bien vestido	b. estar feo
7.	**echar un trago:**	a. comer	b. beber
8.	**hacer acto de presencia:**	a. asistir	b. salir
9.	**para chuparse los dedos:**	a. horrible	b. delicioso
10.	**va por cuenta de la casa:**	a. caro	b. gratis

B. Rewrite the following phrases replacing the italicized word(s) with the appropriate slang synonym(s) from the right column. Make any other necessary changes.

1. ¿Quieres ir a *tomar una bebida* después del trabajo?

   _____

2. Ese tipo *no vale nada.*

   _____

3. ¿Comprendes? Es *claro.*

   _____

4. Huele delicioso. *¡Me está dando hambre!*

   _____

5. ¿Por qué siempre *miente sobre su edad?*

   _____

6. Me gustaría que no *se metiera en lo que no le importa.*

   _____

7. Me cae bien. Parece *buena gente.*

   _____

8. Es increíble como puede hablar *sin parar.*

   _____

9. Es una *linda persona.*

   _____

10. Ella *hace todo por* sus amigos.

    _____

11. ¡Se rió *de mí!*

    _____

12. Creo que ella está intentando *engañarte.*

    _____

A. **dar gato por liebre**

B. **buena onda**

C. **echar un trago**

D. **en mis barbas**

E. **a mil por hora**

F. **ser un cero a la izquierda**

G. **meter la cuchara**

H. **dulzura**

I. **tan claro como el agua**

J. **quitarse los años**

K. **hacérsele agua la boca**

L. **deshacerse por**

C. Complete the phrases by choosing the appropriate word(s) from the list below. Make any necessary changes.

abriles	mil	conservado
barbas	pez	cuenta
anzuelo	mentiras	cuatro
juego	onda	deshacerse

1. Me cae bien. Es buena _____ .

2. Me lo dijo en las _____ .

3. No confío en él. Le conozco el _____ .

4. Más de _____ vienen al Gran Cañón cada año.

5. ¡Qué fiesta tan fantástica! _____ por sus amigos.

6. Está como un _____ en el agua.

7. ¿Tienes solamente 25 _____ ? Estás muy bien _____ .

8. ¿Creíste lo que te dijo? Te tragaste el _____ .

9. ¿Alguna vez has conversado con ella? Habla a _____ por hora.

10. No le creas. Todos sus cuentos son puras _____ .

11. ¡Es gratis! Va por _____ de la casa.

En el trabajo

(At Work)

¡Estoy en ascuas! ¿Qué pasó? He oído decir que la cosa está que arde.

Anda en boca de todos.

Lección tres

EN EL TRABAJO...

DIÁLOGO

Tomás está esperando ansiosamente que David le cuente lo que pasó.

Tomás: ¡Estoy **en ascuas**! ¿Qué pasó? He **oído decir que** la **cosa está que arde**.

David: **Anda en boca de todos**. El jefe estaba **echando chispas** ayer porque Miguel regresó del almuerzo **emborrachado a muerte**. Y **encima de todo**, el jefe lo vio tomando hoy. Lo **cogió con las manos en la masa**.

Tomás: **A que** el jefe no **tiene corazón** para **echarlo a la calle**.

David: Es difícil porque generalmente **hacen buenas migas** y **trabaja de sol a sol**. También tienes que admitir que Miguel **tiene don de gentes**. Además, ¿cómo va a **ganarse la vida**?

Tomás: ¿De qué estás hablando? Miguel siempre **le hace la barba** al jefe. Le **dice amén a todos**. Se me hace raro que **hayan tenido un disgusto** pero ahora Miguel está **fichado** por el jefe.

David: Si me preguntas a mí, yo creo que **el que la hace la paga**. Hacer algo semejante **en pleno** día **no tiene nombre**. ¡Es el **colmo**!

Tomás: Ahora, el jefe lo **tiene pendiente** mientras decide qué hacer con él.

AT WORK...

DIALOGUE

Tomás is waiting impatiently to hear David's news.

Tomás: I'm on pins and needles! What happened? I heard that things are really coming to a head.

David: Everyone's talking about it. The boss was really ticked off yesterday because Miguel came back from lunch dead drunk. And on top of everything else, the boss saw him drinking today. He caught him red-handed.

Tomás: I bet the boss doesn't have the heart to can him.

David: It's hard because they usually get along so well and he does work like a horse. Also, you have to admit that Miguel does have a winning way with people. Besides, how would he make a living?

Tomás: What are you talking about? Miguel keeps buttering up the boss. He's a real yes-man. It seems strange that they had a falling out but now Miguel is on the boss's blacklist.

David: If you ask me, I think it serves him right. Doing something like that in the middle of the day is unbelievable. That's really too much!

Tomás: Now, the boss has Miguel dangling while he decides what to do with him.

Lesson Three

Literal Translation of Dialogue

DIALOGUE

Tomás is anxiously waiting for David to tell him what happened.

Tomás: I'm on coals! What happened? I heard said that the thing is burning.

David: It is in everyone's mouth. The boss was throwing sparks yesterday because Miguel came back from lunch drunk to death. And on top of everything, the boss saw him drinking today. He caught him with the hands in the dough.

Tomás: To that the boss doesn't have the heart to throw him to the street.

David: It's hard because they usually make good crumbs and he does work from sun to sun. Also, you have to admit that Miguel does have a gift of people. Besides, how would he earn his life?

Tomás: What are you talking about? Miguel always shaves the boss's beard. He says Amen to everything. It seems rare to me that they had an argument but now Miguel is filed on a card by the boss.

David: If you ask me, I think he who does it, pays for it. To do something like that in full day doesn't have a name. It's the height.

Tomás: Now, the boss has Miguel dangling while he decides what to do with him.

VOCABULARY

a que *exp.* I'll bet (you) • (lit); to that.

andar en boca de todos *exp.* to have everyone talking about it, to be on everyone's lips • (lit); to go into everyone's mouth.
SYNONYM: **andar en boca de las gentes** *exp.* • (lit); to be in the mouth of the people.

coger a alguien con las manos en la masa *exp.* to catch someone in the act, to catch someone red-handed • (lit); to catch someone with the hands in the dough.
SYNONYM (1): **coger en el acto** *exp.* • (lit); to catch in the act.
SYNONYM (2): **cachar con las manos en la masa** *exp.* • (lit); to seize with the hands in the dough.

colmo *m.* • (lit); height, culmination • *¡Es el colmo!;* That's the limit! (That's the last straw, etc.)

decir amén a todo *exp.* to be a yes-man • (lit); to say Amen to everything.

echar a alguien a la calle *exp.* to fire someone, to can someone • (lit); to throw someone to the street.
SYNONYM: **correr** *v.* • (lit); to run • *Lo corrieron;* He was fired. • NOTE: In this example, the verb *correr* could be loosely translated as "to run someone off."

el que la hace la paga *exp.* what goes around comes around, one must pay the consequences • (lit); he who does it pays for it.

emborracharse a muerte *adv.* to get dead drunk • (lit); to get drunk to death.
SYNONYM: **coger una borrachera** *exp.* • (lit); to catch a drunken state
ANTONYM: **dormir la mona** *exp.* to sleep it off • (lit); to sleep the monkey.
NOTE: **estar crudo** *exp.* to have a hangover • (lit); to be raw • *la cruda;* hangover.

en pleno(a) *adj.* in the middle of • (lit); in full • *¡Los niños estaban jugando en plena calle!;* The children were playing in the middle of the street! • *en pleno día;* in broad daylight.

encima de todo *exp.* on top of everything.

estar echando chispas *exp.* to be hopping mad, to spit fire • (lit); to throw sparks.
ALSO (1): **chispa** *f.* drunkenness • NOTE: **chisparse** *v.* to get drunk • (lit); to "spark up."
ALSO (2): **tener chispa** *exp.* to be witty • (lit); to have spark.

estar fichado(a) *adj.* to be on someone's blacklist • (lit); to be filed on a card, to be indexed.
ALSO: **fichar** *v.* to figure someone out, to have someone's number • *Le tengo bien fichado;* I've got him figured out.

estar sobre/en ascuas *exp.* to be on pins and needles • (lit); to be on embers (or glowing embers).
NOTE: **ascua** *f.* • (lit); live coal.

ganarse la vida *exp.* to earn one's living • (lit); to earn one's life.

hacer buenas migas *exp.* to get along with someone, to hit it off well • (lit); to make good crumbs (together).
ANTONYM: **hacer malas migas** *exp.* not to get along with someone, not to hit it off well • (lit); to make bad crumbs (together).

hacer la barba a alguien *exp.* to butter (someone) up, to kiss up to (somone) • (lit); to shave someone's beard.
ALSO: **reírse en las barbas de uno** *exp.* to laugh in someone's face • (lit); to laugh in someone's beard.

la cosa está que arde *exp.* things are getting hot, things are coming to a head • (lit); the thing is burning • *La cosa está que arde;* Things are coming to a head.
NOTE: **arder** *v.* • (lit); to burn.
ALSO: **arder de/en ira** *exp.* to be furious • (lit); to burn with anger.
SYNONYM (1): **estar hecho una furia** *exp.* • (lit); to become a fury.
SYNONYM (2): **estar como agua para chocolate** *exp.* • (lit); to be like water for chocolate.
SYNONYM (3): **estar hecho un chivo** *exp.* • (lit); to become a kid (young goat).

no tener corazón para *exp.* • (lit); not to have a heart to (do something).
SYNONYM: **ser blando(a) de corazón** *exp.* to be soft-hearted • (lit); to be soft of the heart.
ANTONYM: **tener (el) corazón de piedra** *exp.* to be hardhearted • (lit); to have a heart of stone.
ALSO (1): **tener corazón de pollo** *exp.* to be softhearted • (lit); to have a chicken heart.
ALSO (2): **ser de buen corazón** *exp.* to be kindhearted • (lit); to be of good heart.
ALSO (3): **no tener corazón** *exp.* to be heartless • (lit); not to have (a) heart.

no tener nombre *exp.* to be unspeakable • (lit); not to have a name • *Es tan absurdo que no tiene nombre;* It's so absurd I don't even know what to call it.

oír decir que *exp.* to hear that • (lit); to hear said that.
NOTE: A common mistake made by Spanish students who are trying to say "to hear that" is to say *oír que* instead of *oír decir que*. In the dialogue, the phrase, *He oído decir que es fabulosa,* was used, which literally translates as "I have heard say that it's fabulous." Although the literal translation of *He oído que es fabulosa* is indeed "I have heard that it's fabulous," this would be incorrect Spanish.
SEE: **oír hablar de** *(p. 155)*

tener don de gentes *exp.* to have a winning way (with people) • (lit); to have a gift of people.
NOTE: **gente** *f.* parents, folks • (lit); people • *¿Cómo está tu gente?*; How are your folks?

tener pendiente *exp.* to keep someone hanging (when waiting for news, etc.) • (lit); to keep (someone) hanging.
SYNONYM: **estar pendiente de** *exp.* to be waiting for • (lit); to be hanging.

tener un disgusto *exp.* to have a falling out • (lit); to have an annoyance (or disagreement).

trabajar de sol a sol *exp.* to work like a dog, to work nonstop • (lit); to work from sun to sun.
SYNONYM (1): **trabajar como un mulo** *exp.* • (lit); to work like a mule.
SYNONYM (2): **trabajar como una fiera** *exp.* • (lit); to work like a wild beast.

PRACTICE THE VOCABULARY

[Answers to Lesson 3, p. 54]

A. Complete the phrases by choosing the appropriate word(s) from the list below. Make any necessary changes.

fichado	vida	a muerte
colmo	trabajar	decir
chispas	amén	nombre
disgusto	todo	arde

1. Miguel regresó después del almuerzo emborrachado _____ .
   Y encima de _____ , el jefe lo vio tomando.

2. Enrique está _____ por el jefe.

3. ¿Le robó el dinero? ¡No tiene _____ !

4. He oído _____ que David se va a mudarse.

5. Mi madre estaba echando _____ porque regresó tarde.

6. Estoy cansado porque _____ de sol a sol.

7. La cosa está que _____ .

8. Roberto y David no se hablan porque tuvieron un _____ .

9. Él siempre dice _____ a todo.

10. ¿Cómo se gana la _____ ?

11. ¿Mintió otra vez? ¡Es el _____ !

B. Match the Spanish with the English translation by writing the appropriate letter in the box.

☐ 1. Everyone's talking about it.

☐ 2. I'm on pins and needles!

☐ 3. That's unbelievable.

☐ 4. Jorge has a way with people.

☐ 5. He stole it in broad daylight.

☐ 6. The boss was really ticked off.

☐ 7. He always butters up the teacher.

☐ 8. I caught him red-handed.

☐ 9. Things are really getting hot.

☐ 10. The boss just fired him!

☐ 11. It serves her right.

☐ 12. They get along great.

A. **Siempre le hace la barba al profesor.**

B. **Hacen buenas migas.**

C. **Jorge tiene don de gentes.**

D. **La cosa está que arde.**

E. **Se lo robó en pleno día.**

F. **¡El jefe acaba de echarlo a la calle!**

G. **¡Estoy en ascuas!**

H. **No tiene nombre.**

I. **El que la hace la paga.**

J. **El jefe estaba echando chispas.**

K. **Lo cogió con las manos en la masa.**

L. **Anda en boca de todos.**

C. Underline the appropriate word(s) that best complete(s) the phrase.

1. El jefe lo tiene (**pendencia, pendenciero, pendiente**).

2. He oído (**escuchar, decir, correr**) que Miguel se acaba de casar.

3. ¿Qué pasó? Estoy en (**asceta, ascuas, ascenso**).

4. El que la hace la (**paga, página, paces**).

5. Miguel siempre le hace la (**barbería, barbarie, barba**).

6. ¿Qué hace para ganarse la (**vida, vid, vidalita**)?

7. Jaime tiene (**domo, don, doncella**) de gentes.

8. David y su hermana hacen buenas (**migas, migajas, millas**).

9. Regresó emborrachado a (**muerte, muera, muermo**).

10. Lo cogió con las manos en la (**mesa, masa, mesana**).

11. A (**que, qué, quebrada**) el jefe no tiene (**coraza, corán, corazón**) para echarlo a la (**calle, calma, calina**).

12. ¿Te pidió dinero otra vez? ¡Es el (**colmillo, colocolo, colmo**)!

En el café
(At the Café)

¡Felicidades por tu nuevo café! Brindemos.

Gracias. No quiero echarme flores pero el lugar ya está tomando cuerpo, ¿no crees?

EN EL CAFÉ...

DIÁLOGO

Marco está ayudando a Jaime a celebrar la inauguración de su nuevo café.

Marco: ¡Felicidades por tu nuevo café! **Brindemos**.

Jaime: Gracias. No quiero **echarme flores** pero el lugar ya está **tomando cuerpo**, ¿no crees? ¿De verdad te gusta?

Marco: **¡Por supuesto!** Qué bueno que te hayas **jugado el todo por el todo** y lo hayas comprado. Ya habías dicho que eso era lo que siempre has querido. ¿Qué piensa tu **media naranja** de todo esto?

Jaime: Al principio, le dio **mala espina**. Creo que tuvo que **consultarlo con la almohada**. Después le encantó la idea sobre todo porque salió barato aunque los precios están **por las nubes**. No tuve que **rascarme los bolsillos** demasiado. Hasta pagué **al contado**.

Marco: Si **estuviera en tu pellejo**, estaría **agotado**. Pero sí parece que todo está **saliendo a pedir de boca**.

Jaime: **Fue pan comido** y no **conozco ni jota** de este negocio. Mira, **no me importa un bledo** los pequeños problemas por aquí y por allá. Claro que todavía hay algunos **cabos sueltos**, pero es normal. **Al fin y al cabo**, las cosas serán diferentes ahora que yo **llevo la batuta**.

Marco: **Del dicho al hecho hay mucho trecho**. Seguramente tendrás que **sudar la gota gorda** por un tiempo. Yo sí que no tengo **madera para** ese tipo de trabajo.

AT THE CAFÉ...

DIALOGUE

Marco is helping Jaime celebrate the opening of his new café.

Marco: Congratulations on your new café! Let's drink a toast.

Jaime: Thank you. I don't mean to toot my own horn, but the place is really taking shape, huh? Do you really like it?

Marco: I'll say! It's great that you went for it and bought it. You've said before that it's what you've always wanted. What does your better half have to say about it?

Jaime: At first, it worried her. I think she had to sleep on it. Then she was delighted, especially since it didn't cost much although prices are sky-high. I didn't have to cough up too much. I even paid cash.

Marco: If I were in your shoes, I'd be exhausted. But it does look like everything is working out perfectly.

Jaime: There's nothing to it and I don't know a thing about this business. Listen, I couldn't care less about little problems here and there. Sure there are still a few loose ends but that's normal. When all is said and done, things will be different now that I'm running the show.

Marco: Easier said than done. You may have to work your butt off for a while. I'm sure not cut out for that kind of work.

Literal Translation of Dialogue

DIALOGUE

Marco is helping Jaime celebrate the opening of his new café.

Marco: Congratulations on your new café! Let's toast.

Jaime: Thank you. I don't want to throw myself flowers but the place is now taking shape, don't you think? Do you really like it?

Marco: For supposed! How good that you played everything for everything and bought it. You'd said that it was what you've always wanted. What does your half an orange think about it?

Jaime: At first, it gave her a bad thorn. I believe she had to consult it with the pillow. Later the idea enchanted her especially since it was inexpensive although prices are around the clouds. I didn't have to scratch my pockets too much. I paid counted.

Marco: If I were in your skin, I'd be drained. But it certainly seems like everything is coming out to ask from the mouth.

Jaime: It was like bread eaten and I don't know "J" about this business. Look, it doesn't matter one goosefoot plant to me about little problems here and there. It's clear that there are some loose ends, but it's normal. To the end and the end, things will be different now that I'm carrying the baton.

Marco: From the saying to the doing there is much distance. You will surely have to sweat the fat drop for a time. I certainly don't have the wood for that type of work.

VOCABULARY

al fin y al cabo *exp.* anyway, in the end, after all, when all is said and done • (lit); to the end and the end.
  SYNONYM: **al fin y al fallo** *exp.* (Chile) • (lit); to the end and the judgment.

brindar *exp.* to drink a toast • (lit); to drink in chorus.

cabos sueltos *m.pl.* • (lit); loose ends.

consultarlo con la almohada *exp.* to sleep on it • (lit); to consult it with the pillow.

darle mala espina *exp.* to worry one, to make one feel uneasy • (lit); to give one a bad thorn.

del dicho al hecho hay mucho/gran trecho *exp.* easier said than done • (lit); from the saying to the doing, there is much/great distance.

echarse flores *f.pl.* to toot one's own horn, to flatter oneself • (lit); to throw oneself flowers.
  ALSO: **echarle flores a alguien** *exp.* to flatter someone, to sweet-talk someone • (lit); to throw flowers at someone.

estar agotado(a) *adj.* to be exhausted, be completely tired out • (lit); to be emptied or drained.
  SYNONYM (1): **estar/sentirse como un trapo viejo** *exp.* • (lit); to feel like an old rag.
  SYNONYM (2): **estar rendido** *exp.* • (lit); to be rendered (of all one's energy).
  SYNONYM (3): **estar reventado** *exp.* • (lit); to be burst (like a balloon whose air has suddenly been let out).

estar por las nubes *exp.* to be sky-high • (lit); to be around the clouds.
  ALSO: **ponerse por las nubes** *exp.* to make (prices) soar sky-high • *Los precios se pusieron por las nubes;* The prices were sky-high.

estar/hallarse en el pellejo de otro *exp.* to be in somebody else's shoes • (lit); to be in the skin of another.

jugarse el todo por el todo *exp.* to risk everything, to go for it • (lit); to play (or risk) everything for everything.

llevar la batuta *exp.* to run the show • (lit); to carry the (conductor's) baton.

media naranja *f.* better half, spouse • (lit); **1.** half an orange • **2.** dome, cupola.
  NOTE: In Spanish, a dome is called a *media naranja* or literally, "half an orange" because of its shape. *Media naranja* is commonly used as a humorous and affectionate term for one's spouse since one half completes the other as would two halves of an orange.
  SYNONYM: **mitad** *f* • (lit); half • *mi cara mitad;* my better half.

no importar un bledo *exp.* not to give a darn about (something) • (lit); it doesn't matter one goosefoot plant.

no saber ni jota *exp.* not to know a thing about, not to know beans about • (lit); not to know a "j" about (something).

pagar al contado *exp.* to pay cash • (lit); to pay counted.

por supuesto *exp.* of course, certainly • (lit); for supposed • *¿Hiciste tu tarea? ¡Por supuesto!;* Did you do your homework? Of course!

rascarse el bolsillo *exp.* to cough up money • (lit); to scratch one's pocket.
ALSO: **rascar** *v.* to play the guitar • (lit); to scratch (away at) • **rascatripas** *m.* third-rate violin player.

salir a pedir de boca *exp.* to go perfectly • (lit); to come out to ask from the mouth.
SYNONYM: **salir al pelo** *exp.* to work to a "T" • (lit); to come out to the hair.

ser pan comido *exp.* to be easy, a cinch • (lit); to be eaten bread.

sudar la gota gorda *exp.* to sweat blood, to make a superhuman effort • (lit); to sweat the fat drop.
ALSO (1): **sudar a chorros** *exp.* to sweat like a pig • (lit); to sweat in spurts, gushes, streams, etc.
SYNONYM: **sudar petróleo** *exp.* • (lit); to sweat petroleum.

tener madera para *exp.* to have what it takes, to be cut out for (something) • (lit); to have the wood for something • *Tiene madera para ser papá;* He has what it takes to be a father.
ALSO: **tocar madera** *exp.* to knock on wood • (lit); to touch wood.

tomar cuerpo *m.* 1. to take shape • 2. to thicken (a sauce) • (lit); to take body.

PRACTICE THE VOCABULARY

[Answers to Lesson 4, p. 54]

A. Underline the English translation.

    1. **echarse flores**:   a. to toot one's horn   b. to drink a toast

    2. **llevar la batuta**:   a. to run the show   b. to worry one

3. **sudar la gota gorda**:   a. to sweat blood   b. to sweat a lot

4. **estar agotado**:   a. to be wide awake   b. to be exhausted

5. **por las nubes**:   a. low   b. sky-high

6. **pagar al contado**:   a. to pay on credit   b. to pay cash

7. **ser pan comido**:   a. to be a cinch   b. to be difficult

8. **tener madera para**:   a. to have what it takes   b. to be a real zero

9. **darle mala espina**:   a. to take shape   b. to worry one

10. **salir a pedir de boca**:   a. to be a cinch   b. to go perfectly

B. Fill in the blank with the letter that corresponds to the best choice.

1. –¿Hiciste la cena tú solo? –¡ _____ !
   a. **Por nada**   b. **Por supuesto**   c. **Por las nubes**

2. ¡No me importa un _____ !
   a. **cuerpo**   b. **jota**   c. **bledo**

3. Del dicho al hecho hay mucho _____ .
   a. **trecho**   b. **trebejo**   c. **trazo**

4. Tuve que rascarme el _____ para poder comprar el auto que quería.
   a. **bolsero**   b. **bolo**   c. **bolsillo**

5. Brindemos a _____ .
   a. **coso**   b. **coro**   c. **corro**

6. Va a jugarse el todo por el _____ .
   a. **tocho**   b. **todo**   c. **toga**

7. Todavía hay muchos _____ sueltos.
   a. **cabos**   b. **tornillos**   c. **cabellos**

8. No puedo decidirme. Creo que tengo que consultarlo con la _____ .
   a. **almohaza**   b. **almohadón**   c. **almohada**

9. Me gustaría conocer a tu media _____ .
   a. **naranja**   b. **naranjada**   c. **narcisista**

10. Si yo estuviera en tu _____ , renunciaría.
    a. **pelo**   b. **pellejo**   c. **pellejero**

C. Match the columns by writing the appropriate letter in the box on the left.

☐ 1. I'm exhausted today.

☐ 2. Of course!

☐ 3. Your house is taking shape.

☐ 4. She likes to toot her own horn.

☐ 5. I don't know beans about math.

☐ 6. Just let him run the show.

☐ 7. He has the making of a good father.

☐ 8. When all is said and done, I'm glad we bought the car.

☐ 9. Let's drink a toast.

☐ 10. I have to sleep on it.

☐ 11. Everything went smoothly.

☐ 12. You'll have to pay cash.

☐ 13. The prices in this restaurant are sky-high.

☐ 14. Is this your better half?

A. **Los precios en este restaurante están por las nubes.**

B. **Tiene madera para ser papá.**

C. **Tengo que consultarlo con la almohada.**

D. **Estoy agotado hoy.**

E. **¡Por supuesto!**

F. **Tienes que pagar al contado.**

G. **Al fin y al cabo, me alegro que hayamos comprado el auto.**

H. **Tu casa está tomando cuerpo.**

I. **Todo salió a pedir de boca.**

J. **No sé ni jota de matemáticas.**

K. **A ella le gusta echarse flores.**

L. **Deja que él lleve la batuta.**

M. **Brindemos.**

N. **¿Es ésta tu media naranja?**

En el gran almacén

(In the Department Store)

¡Pero te sienta como anillo al dedo! Te lo digo con el corazón en la mano que se te ve muy bien.

¡Hombre, no me lleves la corriente!

EN EL GRAN ALMACÉN...

DIÁLOGO

Esperanza e Irene han ido de compras.

Esperanza:	Tengo ganas de comprar este vestido pero estoy **nadando entre dos aguas**. Además, **cuesta un ojo de la cara**. Siempre **cargan la mano** aquí y no quiero estar **sin un quinto** durante el resto de la semana.
Irene:	¡Pero te sienta **como anillo al dedo**! Te lo digo **con el corazón en la mano** que se te ve muy bien.
Esperanza:	**¡Hombre**, no me **lleves la corriente**!
Irene:	No, lo digo de verdad. Cuando **te emperifollas** te ves bellísima.
Esperanza:	Si no dejas de **echarme flores** vas a hacer que me **ponga colorada**. De todos modos, **al primer golpe de vista** me gustó pero ahora tengo dudas.
Irene:	Me gustó, pero sobre **gustos no hay nada escrito**.
Esperanza:	¡Ay, mira! Allí está esa vendedora de la cual te estaba hablando. ¡Es tan antipática! La última vez que estuve aquí me insultó **de buenas a primeras**. Después, nos **jalamos de los pelos**.
Irene:	**¿Qué mosca la habrá picado?**
Esperanza:	No **se lleva bien con** nadie. **Se cree la muy muy**.
Irene:	**Un día de estos**, voy a **cantarle las cuarenta**.
Esperanza:	**¡Estoy harta de** ella! Además le está **patinando el coco**. **No tiene pelos en la lengua**. ¡Ay no! ¡Ahí viene! No te preocupes. No me voy a **meter con** ella. Esta vez me voy a **morder la lengua**.

IN THE DEPARTMENT STORE...

DIALOGUE

Esperanza and Irene are out shopping.

Esperanza:	I feel like buying this dress but I just can't make up my mind. Besides, it costs an arm and a leg. They always rip you off here and I don't want to be flat broke for the rest of the week.
Irene:	But it suits you to a T! I'm telling you in all honesty that you look great in it.
Esperanza:	Come on, stop humoring me!
Irene:	No, really! When you get all dressed up, you look beautiful.
Esperanza:	If you don't stop flattering me, you're going to make me blush. Anyway, I did like it at first glance but now I have doubts.
Irene:	I like it but to each his own.
Esperanza:	Oh, look! There's that saleswoman I was telling you about. She's so nasty! That last time I was here, she insulted me right off the bat. Then we had a real fight.
Irene:	What's eating her?
Esperanza:	She just doesn't get along with anyone. She think she's so hot.
Irene:	One of these days I'm going to tell her off.
Esperanza:	I've had it with her. Besides, she's missing a screw. She always says exactly what's on her mind. Oh, no! Here she comes! Don't worry. I won't pick a fight with her. I'll just bite my tongue.

Literal Translation of Dialogue

DIALOGUE

Esperanza and Irene are out shopping.

Esperanza:	I have feelings to buy this dress but I'm swimming between two waters. Besides, it costs an eye from the face. They always charge the hand here and I don't want to be without a fifth for the rest of the week.
Irene:	But it fits you like a ring on a finger. I'm telling you with the heart in the hand that it sees you very well.
Esperanza:	Man, don't carry the current to me!
Irene:	I'm telling you the truth! When you decorate yourself, you're beautiful.
Esperanza:	If you don't stop throwing me flowers, you're going to make me put red. Of all modes, at the first blow of sight I liked it but now I have doubts.
Irene:	I liked it but on tastes there's been nothing written.
Esperanza:	Oh, look! There's that saleswoman I was talking to you about. She's no nasty! The last time I was here she insulted me from the good ones to the first ones. Then we pulled hairs.
Irene:	What fly bit her?
Esperanza:	She doesn't carry herself well with anyone. She thinks she's the very very.
Irene:	One of these days, I'm going to sing her the forty.
Esperanza:	I'm full of her! Besides, she spins her coconut. She doesn't have hairs on the tongue. Oh no! Here she comes! Don't worry. I'm not going to get involved with her. This time I'll just bite the tongue.

VOCABULARY

al primer golpe de vista *exp.* at first glance • (lit); at first stroke/blow/knock of sight.

cantarle las cuarenta *exp.* to tell someone off, to tell someone exactly what's what • (lit); to sing the forty (truths about the person).

cargar la mano *exp.* **1.** to overcharge • **2.** to crack down, to be too strict • **3.** to be heavy-handed with a certain ingredient in a recipe • (lit); to load the hand.
SYNONYM (1): **cargar la cuenta** *exp.* • (lit); to (over)charge the account.
SYNONYM (2): **pasársele la mano** *exp.* • (lit); to pass the hand • *Se le pasa la mano;* He overcharges him/her.

con el corazón en la mano *exp.* in all frankness • (lit); with the heart in the hand.

costar un ojo de la cara *exp.* to cost an arm and a leg • (lit); to cost an eye from the face.
SYNONYM: **costar un huevo** *exp.* (Venezuela, Colombia, Bolivia, Ecuador, Peru) to cost an arm and a leg • (lit); to cost an egg • NOTE: In these countries, the masculine noun *huevo* is commonly used to mean "testicle."

creerse el/la muy muy *exp.* (Mexico) to be conceited, to think highly of oneself • (lit); to believe oneself the very very.
SYNONYM: **creerse la mamá de los pollitos** *exp.* • (lit); to think oneself the mother of the chickens.

de buenas a primeras *exp.* suddenly (and unexpectedly), right off the bat, from the very start • (lit); from the good ones to the first ones.
ALSO: **bueno(a)** *adj.* nasty, bad • (lit); good • *Tiene una buena gripe;* He/She has a nasty flu. •NOTE: This could be compared to the American expression "to have a real good cold" where "real good" actually refers to something that is nasty or disagreeable.
SYNONYM: **luego luego** *adv.* right away • (lit); later later • NOTE: Although its literal translation is indeed "later later," when *luego* is repeated twice, it means, oddly enough, "right away, immediately."

de todos modos *exp.* anyway, at any rate • (lit); in all modes.

echar flores a alguien *exp.* to flatter someone, to soft-soap someone, to butter someone up • (lit); to throw flowers at someone.
SYNONYM (1): **pasar la mano por el lomo** *exp.* • (lit); to pass the hand by the back.
SYNONYM (2): **darle la suave a uno** *exp.* • (lit); to give the soft to someone.
SYNONYM (3): **ser barbero** *exp.* (Mexico) • (lit); to be a barber.
SYNONYM (4): **pasarle la mano a alguien** *exp.* • (lit); to pass one's hand to someone.

emperifollarse *v.* to get all dressed up, to dress to kill • (lit); to decorate or adorn oneself.
SYNONYM (1): **acicalarse** *v.* • (lit); to polish oneself.
SYNONYM (2): **de etiqueta** *exp.* (used only for a man) formal, full dress • (lit); of etiquette, of ceremony • ALSO: **vestirse de etiqueta** *exp.* (used only for a man) to get all dressed up • (lit); to clothe oneself of etiquette.

estar harto(a) de alguien *exp.* • to be fed up with someone, to be sick and tired of someone (lit); to be full of someone.
SYNONYM (1): **alucinar a alguien** *exp.* • (lit); to hallucinate someone •
NOTE: This could be loosely translated as "to see someone in one's worst dreams."
SYNONYM (2): **tener a uno entre cejas** *exp.* • (lit); to have someone between eyebrows.
SYNONYM (3): **tener a uno entre ceja y ceja** *exp.* not to be able to stand someone • (lit); to have someone between eyebrow and eyebrow • ALSO: **estar hasta las cejas de** *exp.* to be fed up with, to have had it up to here • (lit); to be up to the eyebrows with • *Estoy hasta las cejas de mi trabajo;* I've had it with my work.

estar sin un quinto *exp.* to be flat broke • (lit); to be without a fifth.
SYNONYM (1): **brotar el dinero por las orejas (a alguien)** *exp.* • (lit); to sprout money through the ears (of someone).
SYNONYM (2): **estar arrancado(a)** *exp.* • (lit); to be uprooted.
SYNONYM (3): **estar pato** *exp.* (Chile) • (lit); to be duck.
SYNONYM (4): **estar pelado(a)** *exp.* • (lit); to be peeled.
SYNONYM (5): **no tener un real** *exp.* (Spain) • (lit); not to have a *real* (a Spanish coin worth one forth of a peseta).
SYNONYM (6): **no tener un duro** *exp.* (Spain) • (lit); not to have a *duro* (a Spanish dollar).

¡hombre! *interj.* man alive!, come on! • (lit); man.

jalarse de los pelos *exp.* (Mexico) to squabble, to fight • (lit); to pull from one's hairs.

llevarle/seguirle la corriente a uno *exp.* to humor someone • (lit); to carry/ follow the current to someone.

ALSO: **corriente** *adj.* • (lit); flow • **1.** common, ordinary • **2.** cheap • *una mujer corriente;* a cheap woman • NOTE: This comes from the verb *correr* meaning "to run." Therefore, *una corriente* could be loosely translated as "a woman who runs around with more than one man."

llevarse bien con alguien *exp.* to get along well with someone • (lit); to carry oneself well with someone.

ANTONYM: **llevarse mal con alguien** *exp.* not to get along with someone • (lit); to carry oneself badly with someone.

meterse con *exp.* to pick a fight with, to quarrel with • (lit); to put oneself with.

morderse la lengua *exp.* to hold or control one's tongue • (lit); to bite one's tongue.

ANTONYM (1): **no morderse la lengua** *exp.* not to mince words, to speak straight from the shoulder • (lit); not to bite one's tongue.

ANTONYM (2): **cantar claro** *exp.* • (lit); to sing clearly.

ANTONYM (3): **ser claridoso(a)** *exp.* (Venezuela, Central America) • (lit); to be very clear.

nadar entre dos aguas *exp.* to be undecided, on the fence • (lit); to swim between two waters.

SYNONYM (1): **entre azul y buenas noches** *exp.* • (lit); between blue and good night.

SYNONYM (2): **ni un sí ni un no** *exp.* • (lit); not a yes nor a no.

no tener pelos en la lengua *exp.* not to mince one's words, to be outspoken • (lit); not to have hairs on the tongue.

ALSO: **buscar pelos en la sopa** *exp.* to find fault with everything, to nit-pick • (lit); to look for hairs in the soap.

patinarle el coco *exp.* to be missing a screw, to be slipping • (lit); to spin one's coconut.

SYNONYM (1): **traer frito a uno** *exp.* • (lit); to bring fried to someone.

SYNONYM (2): **traer loco a uno** *exp.* • (lit); to bring craziness to someone.

ponerse rojo(a)/colorado(a) *exp.* to blush, to get red in the face • (lit); to put oneself (to become) red.

SYNONYM (1): **acholar(se)** *v.* (Ecuador, Peru) • (lit); to shame (oneself).

SYNONYM (2): **ruborizarse** *v.* (Latin America) • (lit); to make oneself blush.

ALSO (1): **poner rojo/colorado a alguien** *exp.* to make someone blush • (lit); to put someone red.

ALSO (2): **un chiste rojo** *exp.* a dirty joke • (lit); a red joke.

¿qué mosca te pica? *exp.* what's eating you?

sentar como anillo al dedo *exp.* to fit like a glove • (lit); to fit like a ring on a finger.
    ALSO: **venir como anillo al dedo** *exp.* to be just what the doctor ordered, to be just what one was hoping for • (lit); to come like a ring to the finger.

sobre gustos no hay nada escrito *exp.* to each his own (taste) • (lit); on tastes, there is nothing written (meaning: when it comes to tastes, there are no rules).
    SYNONYM: **en gustos se rompen géneros** *exp.* • (lit); in tastes, styles are broken.

un día de estos *exp.* one of these days • (lit); one day of these.

PRACTICE THE VOCABULARY

[Answers to Lesson 5, p. 55]

A. Complete the phrases by choosing the appropriate word(s) from the list below. Make any necessary changes.

golpe de vista	muy muy	colorado
emperifollas	harto	ojo de la cara
flores	mosca	aguas
pelos	anillo	corazón

1. Te sienta como _____ al dedo.

2. No puedo decidir. Estoy nadando entre dos _____ .

3. Se cree la _____ .

4. ¿Qué _____ la habrá picado?

5. Al primer _____ , no me gustó.

6. Si no dejas de echarme _____ vas a molestarme.

7. Te digo con el _____ en la mano que se te ve bien.

8. No tiene _____ en la lengua.

9. Va a hacer que me ponga _____ .

10. Cuesta un _____ .

11. A mí me trae _____ .

12. Cuando te _____ te ves bellísima.

B. Underline the word(s) that best complete(s) the phrases.

1. Cuesta un ojo de la (**carrera, cara, carrerilla**).

2. ¡(**Hombre, Muchacha, Muchacho**), no me lleves la corriente!

3. No me lleves la (**correa, coronilla, corriente**).

4. Además le está patinando el (**cocotal, coco, cóctel**).

5. Sobre gustos no hay nada (**oído, hablado, escrito**).

6. Voy a cantarle las (**veinte, treinta, cuarenta**).

7. La última vez que estuve aquí me insultó de buenas a (**segundas, quintas, primeras**).

8. Tengo ganas de comprar este vestido pero estoy nadando entre (**unos, dos, tres**) aguas.

9. Siempre está jalándose de los (**pelos, pellejeros, pellizcar**) con todos.

10. Se cree el (**poco poco, luego luego, muy muy**).

11. Te lo digo con el corazón en la (**mano, mancera, manaza**).

12. Siempre cargan la (**cabeza, mano, pata**).

C. Match the columns by writing the appropriate letter in the box on the left.

☐ 1. It suits you to a T.

☐ 2. Come on, stop humoring me.

☐ 3. I won't pick a fight with her.

☐ 4. She always says exactly what's on her mind.

☐ 5. I just can't make up my mind.

☐ 6. It costs an arm and a leg.

☐ 7. They always overcharge here.

☐ 8. You're going to make me blush.

☐ 9. I did like it at first glance.

☐ 10. She thinks she's so hot.

☐ 11. When you get all dressed up, you look beautiful.

☐ 12. To each his own.

A. **Vas a hacer que me ponga colorado.**

B. **Sobre gustos no hay nada escrito.**

C. **Te sienta como anillo al dedo.**

D. **Cuando te emperifollas te ves bellísima.**

E. **Hombre, no me sigas llevando corriente.**

F. **Estoy nadando entre dos aguas.**

G. **Cuesta un ojo de la cara.**

H. **Al primer golpe de vista me gustó.**

I. **No me voy a meter con ella.**

J. **Se cree la muy muy.**

K. **No tiene pelos en la lengua.**

L. **Siempre cargan la mano aquí.**

ANSWERS TO LESSONS 1-5

LESSON ONE - *En la escuela*

Practice the Vocabulary

A.
1. tropecé
2. pintura
3. papa
4. vaso
5. Nones
6. chismes
7. paréntesis
8. día
9. nuevo
10. el habla
11. qué
12. oveja

B.
1. espárragos
2. grito en el cielo
3. ligero
4. tomando
5. oído
6. trapo
7. le busca
8. calabazas
9. se pasó
10. clavo
11. coronilla
12. se ahoga

C. **Answers to Word Game**

1. chisme
2. apuro
3. paréntesis
4. clavo
5. día

6. tropezar
7. trapo
8. pinta
9. balde
10. papa

O	P	A	R	T	B	P	U	X	E	P	F
D	M	P	A	R	É	N	T	E	S	I	S
E	M	X	É	R	A	P	D	R	J	N	S
S	C	F	F	E	B	U	A	W	T	T	Y
A	L	R	Y	O	E	Z	J	P	K	A	P
D	A	A	V	I	E	D	B	U	A	R	K
T	V	O	N	P	M	Í	É	G	R	A	U
P	O	E	O	G	O	C	H	I	S	M	E
M	Y	R	M	O	R	M	F	I	E	D	D
D	T	E	G	N	U	E	Y	U	L	U	D
N	B	D	F	E	P	E	J	A	E	W	U
Q	É	W	H	B	A	D	B	E	D	Í	A

D.
1. H
2. D
3. L
4. G
5. K
6. E

7. J
8. B
9. I
10. F
11. C
12. A

LESSON TWO - *En la fiesta*

Practice the Vocabulary

A. 1. b   6. a
   2. a   7. b
   3. b   8. a
   4. b   9. b
   5. a   10. b

B. 1. ¿Quieres ir a echar un trago después del trabajo?
   2. Ese tipo es un cero a la izquierda.
   3. ¿Comprendes? Es tan claro como el agua.
   4. Huele delicioso. ¡Se me hace agua la boca!
   5. ¿Por qué siempre se quita los años?
   6. Me gustaría que no metiera la cuchara.
   7. Me cae bien. Parece buena onda.
   8. Es increíble como puede hablar a mil por hora.
   9. Es una dulzura.
   10. Ella se deshace por sus amigos.
   11. ¡Se rió en mis barbas!
   12. Creo que ella está intentando darte gato por liebre.

C. 1. onda   7. abriles; conservado
   2. barbas   8. anzuelo
   3. juego   9. mil
   4. cuatro   10. mentiras
   5. Se deshace   11. cuenta
   6. pez

LESSON THREE - *En el trabajo*

Practice the Vocabulary

A. 1. a muerte; todo
   2. fichado
   3. nombre
   4. decir
   5. chispas
   6. trabajo
   7. arde
   8. disgusto
   9. amén
   10. vida
   11. colmo

B. 1. L
   2. G
   3. H
   4. C
   5. E
   6. J
   7. A
   8. K
   9. D
   10. F
   11. I
   12. B

C. 1. pendiente
   2. decir
   3. ascuas
   4. paga
   5. barba
   6. vida
   7. don
   8. migas
   9. muerte
   10. mesa
   11. que; corazón; calle
   12. colmo

LESSON FOUR - *En el café*

Practice the Vocabulary

A. 1. a
   2. a
   3. a
   4. b
   5. b
   6. b
   7. a
   8. a
   9. b
   10. b

B. 1. b
    2. c
    3. a
    4. c
    5. b

    6. b
    7. a
    8. c
    9. a
    10. b

C. 1. D
    2. E
    3. H
    4. K
    5. J
    6. L
    7. B

    8. G
    9. M
    10. C
    11. I
    12. F
    13. A
    14. N

LESSON FIVE - *En el gran almacén*

Practice the Vocabulary

A. 1. anillo
    2. aguas
    3. muy muy
    4. mosca
    5. golpe de vista
    6. flores

    7. corazón
    8. pelos
    9. colorado
    10. ojo de la cara
    11. harto
    12. emperifollas

B. 1. cara
    2. Hombre
    3. corriente
    4. coco
    5. escrito
    6. cuarenta

    7. primeras
    8. dos
    9. pelos
    10. muy muy
    11. mano
    12. mano

C. 1. C
    2. E
    3. I
    4. K
    5. F
    6. G

    7. L
    8. A
    9. H
    10. J
    11. D
    12. B

REVIEW EXAM FOR LESSONS 1-5

[Answers to Review Exam, p. 62]

A. Underline the correct definition for the word(s) in boldface.

1. **estar en un apuro:**
   a. to be fed up
   b. to be in a jam
   c. to be exhausted

2. **chisme:**
   a. juicy piece of gossip
   b. nice guy
   c. nasty woman

3. **entre paréntesis:**
   a. strange
   b. quietly
   c. by the way

4. **estar hasta la coronilla:**
   a. to cut class
   b. to be fed up
   c. to be exhausted

5. **ser muy ligero de palabra:**
   a. to be shy
   b. to be extroverted
   c. to be talkative

6. **dar gato por liebre:**
   a. to deceive
   b. to be speechless
   c. to chat

7. **tener malas pulgas:**
   a. to be ill-tempered
   b. to be happy
   c. to be sad

8. **poner el grito en el cielo:**
   a. to party
   b. to drink
   c. to scream

9. **estar bien conservado:**
   a. to be well-preserved   b. to be energetic   c. to be talkative

10. **echar un trago:**
    a. to be angry   b. to be happy   c. to have a drink

11. **en las barbas:**
    a. to get a haircut   b. in one's face   c. in one's back

12. **ir de parranda:**
    a. to go partying   b. to go shopping   c. to be energetic

13. **meter la cuchara:**
    a. to eat   b. to fight   c. to butt in

14. **más de cuatro:**
    a. several people   b. a little   c. large dinner

B. Complete the sentences by choosing the appropriate words from the list below.

tropecé	día	grito
ahoga	espárragos	papa
coronilla	ojos	cuenta
barbas	anzuelo	agua

1. Ponme al _____ .

2. No entiendo ni _____ .

3. Siempre se _____ en un vaso de agua.

4. Va por _____ de la casa.

5. !Dichosos los _____ !

6. Puso el _____ en el cielo.

7. _____ con Ana en la calle.

8. Me lo dijo en las _____ .

9. Se me hace _____ la boca.

10. Te tragaste el _____ .

11. El profesor está hasta la _____ de ella.

12. La voy a mandar a freír _____ .

C. Match the English with the Spanish.

☐ 1. How nice to see you.

☐ 2. He's only thirty years old.

☐ 3. He always butts into other people's business.

☐ 4. It's delicious.

☐ 5. Things are getting hot.

☐ 6. Everyone's talking about it.

☐ 7. They get along well.

☐ 8. He always butters up the boss.

☐ 9. It worried her.

☐ 10. Let's drink a toast.

☐ 11. She needed to sleep on it.

☐ 12. I'm not cut out for that kind of work.

A. **Siempre mete la cuchara en lo que no le importa.**

B. **La cosa está que arde.**

C. **Hacen buenas migas.**

D. **Siempre le hace la barba al jefe.**

E. **Solamente tiene treinta abriles.**

F. **Brindemos a coro.**

G. **Le dió mala espina.**

H. **No tengo madera para ese tipo de trabajo.**

I. **Ella tuvo que consultarlo con la almohada.**

J. **Dichosos los ojos.**

K. **Anda en boca de todos.**

L. **Está para chuparse los dedos.**

D. Underline the appropriate word(s) that best complete(s) each sentence.

1. Creo que es buenísimo que te jugaste el todo por el (**torro, trecho, todo**).

2. ¿Qué piensa tu media (**naranja, narizota, naranjada**) de todo esto?

3. El costo no estuvo por las (**novias, nubes, nueces**).

4. No tuve que rascarme los (**bolsitas, bolleros, bolsillos**) demasiado.

5. Todo está saliendo a pedir de (**boca, cara, cabeza**).

6. Fue (**bizcocho, estofado, pan**) comido.

7. Las cosas serán diferentes ahora que yo llevo la (**baturrillo, batidera, batuta**).

8. Del dicho al hecho hay mucho (**trebejo, trecho, trabajo**).

9. No tengo (**madera, madeja, machota**) para ser papá.

10. Se cree el (**muy muy, luego luego, grande grande**).

11. Cuesta (**una nariz, una boca, un ojo**) de la cara.

12. Está jalándose de (**las pellejas, las pellejerías, los pelos**) con todos.

E. Underline the correct synonym for the word(s) in boldface.

1. **cargar la mano:**
   a. el corazón en la mano   b. de etiqueta   c. pasar la mano

2. **de buenas a primeras:**
   a. poco poco   b. muy muy   c. luego luego

3. **agotado:**
   a. como un trapo viejo   b. tomar cuerpo   c. echarse flores

4. **emborracharse a muerte:**
   a. coger una borrachera   b. estar que arde   c. estar fichado

5. **coger con las manos en la masa:**
   a. en el colmo   b. en el acto   c. en las migas

6. **echar a alguien a la calle:**
   a. hacer la barba   b. estar agotado   c. correr

7. **parranda:**
   a. chisme   b. gala   c. parrandeo

8. **chisme:**
   a. chispazo   b. chispa   c. chispero

9. **hasta la coronilla:**
   a. hasta la punta del pelo   b. perder el habla   c. pasarse la raya

10. **poner al día:**
    a. poner como un trapo   b. poner verde   c. poner al corriente

F. **FIND-THE-WORD CUBE.** First, fill in the blanks with the correct word using words from the list below. Then find and circle the word in the grid on page 61. The first one has been done for you.

boca	vida	pintura
clavo	pulgas	anzuelo
trago	barbas	dedos
cuatro	trapo	chispas
papa	migas	tornillo

1. **faltar un** ___*tornillo*___ *exp.* to be crazy, to have a screw loose.

2. **no entiendo ni** _____ *exp.* not to understand a thing.

3. **dar en el** _____ *exp.* to hit the nail on the head.

4. **no poder ver a uno ni en** _____ *exp.* not to be able to stand someone.

5. **poner a uno como un** _____ *exp.* to rake someone over the coals.

6. **tener malas** _____ *exp.* to be irritable, ill-tempered.

7. **echar un** _____ *exp.* to have a drink.

8. **en las** _____ *exp.* in one's face.

9. **para chuparse los** _____ *exp.* delicious.

10. **más de** _____ *exp.* several people.

11. **tragarse el** _____ *exp.* to swallow something hook, line, and sinker.

12. **estar echando** _____ *exp.* to be hopping mad.

13. **ganarse la** _____ *exp.* to earn one's living.

14. **hacer buenas** _____ *exp.* to get along with someone, to hit it off well.

15. **a pedir de** _____ *exp.* to go smoothly.

FIND-THE-WORD CUBE

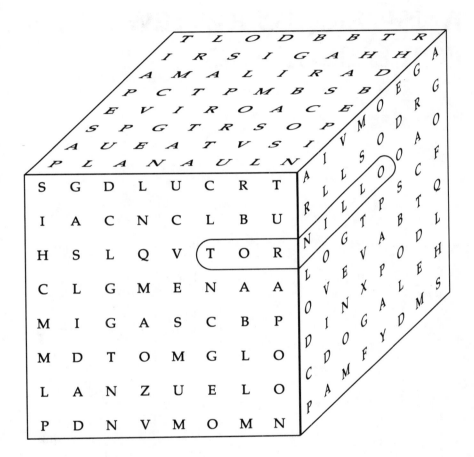

ANSWERS TO REVIEW EXAM FOR LESSONS 1-5

A.
1. b
2. a
3. c
4. b
5. c
6. a
7. a
8. c
9. a
10. c
11. b
12. a
13. c
14. a

B.
1. día
2. papa
3. ahoga
4. cuenta
5. ojos
6. grito
7. Tropecé
8. barbas
9. agua
10. anzuelo
11. coronilla
12. espárragos

C.
1. J
2. E
3. A
4. L
5. B
6. K
7. C
8. D
9. G
10. F
11. I
12. H

D.
1. todo
2. naranja
3. nubes
4. bolsillos
5. boca
6. pan
7. batuta
8. trecho
9. madera
10. muy muy
11. un ojo
12. los pelos

E.
1. c
2. c
3. a
4. a
5. b
6. c
7. c
8. a
9. a
10. c

F. Answers to the FIND-THE-WORD CUBE

1. tornillo
2. papa
3. clavo
4. pintura
5. trapo
6. pulgas
7. trago
8. barbas
9. dedos
10. cuatro
11. anzuelo
12. chispas
13. vida
14. migas
15. boca

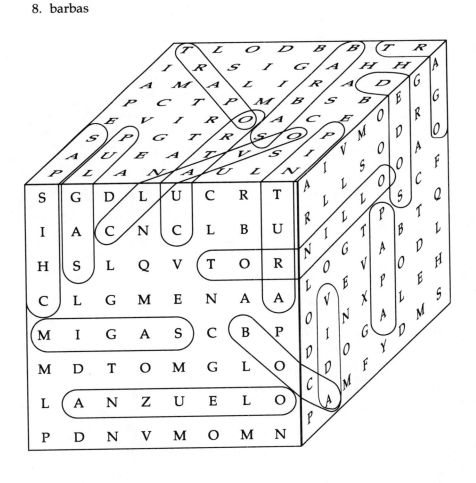

LESSON SIX

Los nuevos vecinos

(The New Neighbors)

Hoy conocí a los nuevos vecinos. Decidí ir a romper el hielo.

Bueno, entonces, vamos al asunto. Cuéntame todo sin faltar una coma.

Lección seis

LOS NUEVOS VECINOS...

DIÁLOGO

Susana está conversando con Cuquita sobre los nuevos vecinos.

Susana: Hoy **conocí** a los nuevos vecinos. Decidí ir a **romper el hielo**.

Cuquita: Bueno, entonces, vamos **al asunto**. Cuéntame todo **sin faltar una coma**. ¿Cómo son?

Susana: Cuando llegué, estaban **gritando como unos descosidos**. Habían **perdido los estribos**. Ella estaba **echando espumarajos** por la boca porque él no **quiso mover un dedo** y ella tuvo que desempacar todo. Así que ofrecí **darles una mano. En fin**, primero **hicieron mal papel**, pero ahora todo parece estar bien.

Cuquita: ¿Qué tipo de cosas tienen?

Susana: No mucho. Hasta hace poco, estaban **más pobres que una rata**.

Cuquita: ¡Qué horrible tener que **vivir al día**! **Gracias a Dios** se están poniendo **a flote** otra vez.

Susana: Ahora tienen uno que otro cuadro, algunas plantas, cosas **por el estilo**. De cualquier manera, es obvio que ella **lleva los pantalones** en la familia. Pero ése es **otro cantar**. Él es profesor y creo que es un **pez gordo**.

Cuquita: ¿Cómo es él?

Susana: **No inventó la pólvora**. Pero llevan muchos años de casados. Él debe tener un **no sé qué**. Y tienen una hija bonita que es **escupida de** su madre y, aparentemente, un **ratón de biblioteca**. Anda **cosida a las faldas de su mamá**. ¡Ah! Y acaba de **dar a luz a** un bebé.

THE NEW NEIGHBORS...

DIALOGUE

Susana is talking with Cuquita about the new neighbors.

Susana: I met the new neighbors today. I decided to go over and break the ice.

Cuquita: Well then, let's get down to the facts. Tell me everything down to the last detail. What are they like?

Susana: When I first got there, they were shouting at the top of their lungs. They had really lost it. She was ticked off because he didn't want to lift a finger and she was stuck doing all the unpacking herself. So I volunteered to lend them a hand. In short, at first they made a lousy impression, but now everything seems okay.

Cuquita: What kind of things do they own?

Susana: Not a lot. Until recently, they were stone-broke.

Cuquita: How awful to have to live from hand to mouth like that! Thank heaven they're getting back on their feet again.

Susana: Now they have a few paintings, some plants, things of that sort. Anyway, it's obvious that she wears the pants in the family. But that's another story. He's a teacher and I think he's a bigwig.

Cuquita: What's he like?

Susana: He's no genius. But they've been married for many years. He must have a certain something. And they have a pretty daughter who's the spit and image of her mother and, evidently, a real bookworm. She's really tied to her mother's apron strings. Oh! And she just gave birth to a baby.

Literal Translation of Dialogue

DIALOGUE

Susana is conversing with Cuquita about the new neighbors.

Susana: Today I knew the new neighbors. I decided to go break the ice.

Cuquita: Well, then, let's go to the subject. Tell me everything without missing a comma. What are they like?

Susana: When I first arrived, they were screaming like something unstitched. They had lost the stirrups. She was throwing foam from the mouth because he didn't want to move a finger and she had to unpack everything. So I offered to give them a hand. To the end, first they did bad role, but now everything seems well.

Cuquita: What type of things do they have?

Susana: Not much. Until recently, they were poorer than a rat.

Cuquita: How horrible to have to live to the day! Thanks to God they're putting themselves afloat again.

Susana: Now they have some paintings, some plants, things for the style. Of any manner, it's obvious that she wears the pants in the family. But that's another song. He is a professor and I think he's a fat fish.

Cuquita: What's he like?

Susana: He didn't invent gunpowder. But they carry many years of marriage. He must have an I-don't-know-what. And they have a beautiful daughter who is the spit of her mother and, evidently, a library mouse. She's sewn to the skirts of her mother. Oh! And they just gave light to a baby.

VOCABULARY

conocer *v.* to meet • (lit); to know.
NOTE: This usage of *conocer* is extremely popular throughout the Spanish-speaking communities.

dar a luz a *exp.* **1.** to give birth to • **2.** to publish • (lit); to give light to.
ALSO: **en plena luz** *exp.* in broad daylight • (lit); in full light.

echar espumarajos por la boca *exp.* to be furious, to foam at the mouth with rage • (lit); to throw foam from the mouth.
SYNONYM: **enchilarse** *v.* (Mexico) • (lit); to get red in the face from eating chilies.

echarle una mano a uno *exp.*to lend someone a hand • (lit); to throw someone a hand.
SYNONYM: **dar una mano** *exp.* • (lit); to give a hand.

en fin *exp.* in short • (lit); in the end • *En fin, es estúpido;* In short, he's stupid.

estar cosido(a) a las faldas de *exp.* to be tied to the apron strings of • (lit); to be sewn to the skirts of.
ALSO: **andar siempre entre faldas** *exp.* to be always with the girls • (lit); to go always with skirts.

gritar como un descosido *exp.* to scream one's lungs out, to scream out of control • (lit); to scream like something unstitched.
NOTE: This expression comes from the verb *descoser* meaning "to unstitch." Therefore, this expression could be loosely translated as "to come apart at the seams."
ALSO: **beber/comer/correr como un descosido** *exp.* to drink/eat/run like crazy.

hacer mal/buen papel *exp.* to make a bad/good impression • *Hiciste buen papel anoche;* You made a good impression last night • (lit); to do a bad/good (theatrical) role.

ir al asunto *exp.* to get down to the facts • (lit); to go to the subject.

llevar los pantalones *exp.* to wear the pants • (lit); to wear the pants.
SYNONYM: **llevar los calzones** *exp.* • (lit); to wear the trousers.

no haber inventado la pólvora *exp.* to be no genius, to be thick-skinned • (lit); not to have invented gunpowder.
ALSO: **gastar (la) pólvora en salvas** *exp.* to waste one's efforts • (lit); to waste gunpowder in vollies.

no mover un dedo *exp.* not to lift a finger • (lit); not to move a finger.

perder los estribos *exp.* to lose control, to lose one's head, to lose one's temper • (lit); to lose the stirrups.

pez gordo *exp.* person of importance, "bigwig" • (lit); fat fish.
SYNONYM: **de peso** *exp.* • (lit); of weight, weighty • *Ese señor es una persona de peso;* That man's a bigwig.

ponerse a flote *exp.* to get back up on one's own two feet again • (lit); to put oneself afloat.
SYNONYM: **levantar cabeza** *exp.* • (lit); to lift the head • NOTE: This could best be compared to the American expression, "to hold up one's head" or "to pull oneself back up."

por el estilo *exp.* of that sort • (lit); in the style • **1.** *En el fuego, perdí una televisión, un piano y cosas por el estilo;* In the fire, I lost a television, a piano, and things of that sort • **2.** *Me dijo que era profesor o algo por el estilo;* He told me he was a teacher or something like that.

ratón de biblioteca *exp.* bookworm • (lit); library mouse.

romper el hielo *exp.* • (lit); to break the ice.
ALSO: **estar hecho un hielo** *exp.* to be frozen, to be freezing cold • (lit); to have become an ice.

ser escupida de *exp.* to be the spit and image of • (lit); to be the spit of.
NOTE: *Es escupida de su madre;* (lit); She's the spit of her mother [or] *Es su madre escupida;* (lit) It's her mother spit (out).

ser más pobre que una rata *exp.* to be stone-broke • (lit); to be as poor as a rat.
NOTE: This could best be compared to the American expression, "to be as poor as a church mouse."
ALSO: **rata/ratero(a)** *n.* thief.
SYNONYM: **pelado(a)** *adj.* • (lit); peeled.

ser otro cantar *exp.* to be another story • (lit); to be another song.
SYNONYM (1): **ser harina de otro costal** *exp.* • (lit); to be flour of a different sack • *Eso es harina de otro costal;* That's a different story.
SYNONYM: **no viene al cuento** *exp.* • (lit); it doesn't come to the story.

sin faltar una coma *exp.* down to the last detail • (lit); without missing a comma.
   SYNONYM: **con puntos y comas** *exp.* • (lit); with periods and commas.

un no sé qué *exp.* a certain something, "je ne sais quoi" • (lit); an "I-don't-know-what."

vivir al día *exp.* to live from hand to mouth • (lit); to live to the day.
   ALSO: **poner al día** *exp.* to bring up-to-date • (lit); to put to the day.

PRACTICE THE VOCABULARY

[Answers to Lesson 6, p. 120]

A. Complete the phrases by choosing the appropriate word(s) from the list below. Make any necessary changes.

faldas	luz	no sé qué
asunto	descosidos	papel
dedo	pólvora	flote
escupida	rata	hielo

1. Soy más pobre que una _____ .

2. Anda cosida a las _____ de su mamá.

3. Acaba de dar a _____ a un bebé.

4. Es _____ de su madre.

5. Él debe tener un _____ .

6. Voy a conocer a los nuevos vecinos y romper el _____ .

7. A ver, vamos al _____ .

8. Él no movió un _____ y ella tuvo que desempacar todo.

9. Con respecto a su inteligencia, él no inventó la _____ .

10. Cuando llegué, estaban gritando como unos _____ .

11. Primero hicieron mal _____ , pero ahora todo parece estar bien.

12. Gracias a Dios se están poniendo a _____ otra vez.

B. Underline the word(s) in parentheses that best complete(s) the sentence.

1. Decidí ir a romper el (**hielo, ratón, día**).

2. Le gusta leer todo el tiempo. Aparentemente es un (**rato, raticida, ratón**) de biblioteca.

3. Cuéntame todo sin faltar una (**coma, como, come**).

4. Cuando llegué, estaban gritando como unos (**ratos, descosidos, estribos**).

5. Habían perdido los (**estribos, estribillos, estridores**).

6. Es obvio que ella lleva los (**zapatos, cinturones, pantalones**) en la familia.

7. Ofrecí darle una (**mano, cabeza, pierna**).

8. Ella estaba echando (**espumaderas, espumarajos, esputos**) por la boca porque él no quería mover un (**braso, dedo, nariz**).

9. ¡Qué horrible tener que vivir (**a la semana, al mes, al día**)!

10. Uno que otro cuadro, algunas plantas, cosas por el (**estribo, espumarajo, estilo**).

C. Match the columns.

☐ 1. She just gave birth to a baby.

☐ 2. Let's get down to the facts.

☐ 3. I decided to go over and break the ice.

☐ 4. Thank God they're getting back on their feet.

☐ 5. They were shouting at the top of their lungs.

☐ 6. That's another story.

☐ 7. He's no genius.

A. **Es obvio que ella lleva los pantalones en la familia.**

B. **Estaban gritando como unos descosidos.**

C. **Ofrecí echarles una mano.**

D. **Ella acaba de dar a luz a un bebé.**

E. **Ella estaba echando espumarajos por la boca.**

F. **Creo que es un pez gordo.**

☐ 8. I think he's a big wig.

☐ 9. It's obvious that she wears the pants in the family.

☐ 10. Tell me everything down to the last detail.

☐ 11. She was ticked off.

☐ 12. I volunteered to lend them a hand.

G. **Vamos al asunto.**

H. **Decidí ir a romper el hielo.**

I. **Gracias a Dios que se están poniendo a flote otra vez.**

J. **No inventó la pólvora.**

K. **Cuéntame todo sin faltar una coma.**

L. **Ése es otro cantar.**

El huésped

(The House Guest)

Creí que iba a quedarse unos días y después iba a largarse.

Yo también. Anda como Pedro por su casa. Tenga ganas de romperle la crisma.

Lección siete

EL HUÉSPED...

DIÁLOGO

Rafael está ayudando a Carlos a resolver un problema.

Carlos: Estaba **pensando para mis adentros** que podría pedirle que se fuera **en el acto** pero soy demasiado **blando de corazón**.

Rafael: Tienes que hacer algo o se va a quedar aquí para siempre.

Carlos: **¡Dios me libre!** Estoy **harto** de él. Se me **pega como una ladilla**. No solamente eso pero ayer **hizo añicos** mi florero favorito. Estaba dispuesto a **pasar por alto** algunas de las cosas que ha hecho pero sinceramente, no sé cómo **me las he arreglado para** aguantarlo tanto tiempo.

Rafael: Creí que iba a quedarse unos días y después iba a **largarse**.

Carlos: Yo también. Anda **como Pedro por su casa**. Tengo ganas de **romperle la crisma**.

Rafael: **En buen lío** te has metido.

Carlos: Al principio, lo recibí **con los brazos abiertos** y ahora **estoy a dos dedos de** gritar. **No es cosa de juego**. ¡Tengo los **nervios de punta**! **No sé dónde meterme**.

Rafael: No quiero **meter las narices en** lo que no me importa pero **a todas luces**, tienes que pedirle que se vaya. **¡No des el brazo a torcer!** Tienes que **mirar por tus intereses**.

Carlos: Yo sé. Tengo que **deshacerme** de él sin **partirle el corazón**.

Rafael: **Párrafo aparte**, ¿come mucho?

Carlos: **¡Come como un desfondado!**

THE HOUSE GUEST...

DIALOGUE

Rafael is helping Carlos solve a problem.

_____

Carlos: I was thinking to myself that I could just ask him to leave right away, but I'm just too soft-hearted.

Rafael: Well, you'd better do something or he'll stay here forever.

Carlos: Heaven forbid! I'm fed up with him. He sticks to me like a leech. Not only that, but yesterday he smashed my favorite vase to smithereens. I was willing to overlook some of the things he did but frankly, I don't know how I've managed to put up with him this long.

Rafael: I thought he was going to stay for a few days and then he'd take off.

Carlos: Me too. He acts as if he owned the place. I feel like ringing his neck.

Rafael: You've gotten yourself into a real mess.

Carlos: At first, I welcomed him with open arms and now I'm on the verge of screaming. It's no laughing matter. My nerves are on edge! I don't know where to turn.

Rafael: I don't want to stick my nose in other people's business, but no matter how you look at it, you just have to ask him to leave. Stick to your guns on this! You've got to look out for number one.

Carlos: I know. I have to get rid of him without breaking his heart.

Rafael: Not to change the subject, but does he eat a lot?

Carlos: He eats like a pig!

Literal Translation of Dialogue

DIALOGUE

Rafael is helping Carlos resolve a problem.

_____

Carlos: I was thinking to my insides that I could ask him to leave in the act but I'm too soft of the heart.

Rafael: Well, you have to do something or he'll stay here forever.

Carlos: God free me! I'm full of him. He sticks to me like a crab louse. Not only that but yesterday he made fragments out of my favorite vase. I was ready to pass for high some of the things he did but honestly, I don't know how I've arranged to put up with him for such a long time.

Rafael: I thought he was going to stay for a few days and then let go.

Carlos: Me too. He acts like Pedro through his house. I have desires to break his baptism.

Rafael: You got yourself into a good bundle.

Carlos: At first, I received him with open arms and now I'm at two fingers from screaming. It's not a game thing. I have nerves to the tip! I don't know where to put myself.

Rafael: I don't want to put the noses in that which doesn't concern me but by all lights, you have to ask him to leave. Don't give the arm to twist! You have to look out for your interests.

Carlos: I know. I have to undo myself of him without breaking his heart.

Rafael: Paragraph aside, does he eat a lot?

Carlos: He eats like something without a bottom!

VOCABULARY

a todas luces *exp.* any way you look at it, clearly • (lit); by all lights.
    ALSO: **de pocas luces** *exp.* stupid, dim-witted • (lit); of little lights • NOTE:
This could best be compared to the American expression, "The lights are on
but nobody's home."
    SYNONYM: **a toda luz** *exp.* • (lit); by all light.

arreglárselas para *exp.* to manage to • (lit); to arrange oneself by.
    ALSO: **¡Ya te arreglaré!** *exp.* I'll fix you!, I'll get even with you! • (lit); I'll
arrange you!

comer como un desfondado *exp.* to eat like a pig • (lit); to eat as if one's bottom
fell off.
    NOTE: The noun *desfondado* comes from the verb *desfondar·*meaning "to go
through or break the bottom of."

como Pedro por su casa *exp.* as if he owned the place • (lit); like Peter in his
house.

con los brazos abiertos *exp.* • (lit); with open arms.
    ALSO: **estar hecho un brazo de mar** *exp.* to be dressed to kill • (lit); to be made
an arm to the sea.

deshacerse de *v.* to get rid of • (lit); to undo oneself of.
    ALSO: **deshacerse por (uno)** *exp.* to go out of one's way for someone, to outdo
oneself for • SEE: *Lesson Two – Vocabulary*, p. 17.

¡Dios me libre! *interj.* God forbid! • (lit); God free me!
    SYNONYM: **¡Vaya por Dios!** *exp.* • Good God! (lit); Go by God!

en el acto *exp.* **1.** immediately, on the spot • **2.** in the act (of doing something)
• (lit); in the act.
    SYNONYM: **acto continuo/seguido** *exp.* • (lit); continuous/consecutive act.

estar a dos dedos de *exp.* to be on the verge of • (lit); to be two fingers from.
    SYNONYM: **dedo** *m.* a little bit • (lit); finger • *Beber un dedo de vino;* To drink
a drop of wine.

estar harto(a) de alguien *exp.* to be fed up with someone • (lit); to be satiated
with.
    SYNONYM: **tenerle a uno hasta en la sopa** *exp.* to have one satiated in soup.

hacer añicos *exp.* **1.** (of objects) to smash to smithereens • **2.** (of paper) to rip
to shreds • (lit); to make (into) fragments or bits.
    ALSO: **estar hecho añicos** *exp.* to be worn out, exhausted • (lit); to be made
into fragments or bits.

largarse *v.* to leave • (lit); to loosen, to let go, to set free.

meter las narices en lo que a uno no le importa *exp.* to butt into other people's business, to poke (to stick) one's nose into everything • (lit); to put the nose into that which doesn't concern one.
ALSO: **en sus mismas narices** *exp.* right under one's very nose • (lit); in one's own nose.

meterse en buen lío *exp.* to get oneself into a fine mess • (lit); to put oneself in a good bundle.

mirar por sus intereses *exp.* to look out for oneself, to look out for number one • (lit); to look out for one's interests.
ALSO: **mirar bien/mal a uno** *exp.* to like/dislike someone • (lit); to look someone well/badly.

no dar el brazo a torcer *exp.* to stick to one's guns, not to give in, not to have one's arm twisted • (lit); not to give one's arm to be twisted.
ANTONYM: **dar el brazo a torcer** *exp.* to give in, to have one's arm twisted • (lit); to give one's arm to be twisted.

no saber dónde meterse *exp.* not to know where to turn • (lit); not to know where to put oneself.

no ser cosa de juego *exp.* to be no laughing matter • (lit); not to be a thing of game.
ALSO: **hacer doble juego** *exp.* to be two-faced • (lit); to make double game.

párrafo aparte *exp.* not to change the subject but • (lit); paragraph aside.

partirle el corazón a uno *exp.* • (lit); to break someone's heart.

pasar por alto *exp.* to ignore, overlook, or pass over • (lit); to pass for tall.

pegársele como una ladilla *exp.* (somewhat vulgar, use with discretion) to stick to someone like glue • (lit); to stick to someone like a crab (as in pubic lice).
ALSO: **pegarle cuatro gritos a alguien** *exp.* to give someone a piece of one's mind, to rake someone over the coals • (lit); to let out four screams to someone.

pensar para sus adentros *exp.* to think to oneself • (lit); to think by one's insides.

romperle la crisma a alguien *exp.* to break someone's head • (lit); to break one's chrism.
SYNONYM (1): **romperle el bautismo** *exp.* • (lit); to break one's baptism.
SYNONYM (2): **romperle la cara (a alguien)** *exp.* to smash someone's face • (lit); to break someone's face.
NOTE: **crisma** *f.* head • (lit); chrism.

ser blando(a) de corazón *exp.* to be soft-hearted • (lit); to be soft of the heart.
ALSO: **blando(a)** *adj.* easy • (lit); soft • *Una vida blanda;* An easy life.
ANTONYM: **tener corazón de piedra** *exp.* to be hard-hearted • (lit); to have a heart of stone.

tener los nervios de punta *exp.* to be edgy • (lit); to have one's nerves on end.
SYNONYM: **estar hecho un manojo de nervios** *exp.* to be a bundle of nerves • (lit); to be made a bundle of nerves.

PRACTICE THE VOCABULARY

[Answers to Lesson 7, p. 121]

A. Choose the expression in the second column that matches the definition on the left.

1. _____ *exp.* to get oneself into a fine mess

2. _____ *exp.* to stick to one's guns, not to give in

3. _____ *exp.* to break someone's heart

4. _____ *exp.* to be fed up with someone

5. _____ *exp.* to be on the verge of

6. _____ *exp.* as if he owned the place

7. _____ *exp.* immediately

8. _____ *exp.* to stick to someone like glue

9. _____ *exp.* to butt into other people's business

10. _____ *exp.* to smash to smithereens

11. _____ *exp.* to leave

12. _____ *exp.* to manage to

A. **largarse**

B. **hacer añicos**

C. **meterse en buen lío**

D. **arreglárselas para**

E. **meter las narices en lo que a uno no le importa**

F. **partirle el corazón a uno**

G. **en el acto**

H. **no dar el brazo a torcer**

I. **como Pedro por su casa**

J. **estar a dos dedos de**

K. **estar harto de alguien**

L. **pegársele como una ladilla**

B. Fill in the blanks with the appropriate letter.

1. Soy demasiado _____ de corazón.
    a. **blanco**   b. **blando**   c. **blancote**

2. Lo recibí con los _____ abiertos.
    a. **brazos**   b. **brazuelos**   c. **braserillos**

3. Estoy a _____ dedos de gritar.
    a. **dos**   b. **tres**   c. **cuatro**

4. _____ aparte, ¿come mucho?
    a. **Frase**   b. **Oración**   c. **Párrafo**

5. Anda como _____ por su casa.
    a. **Miguel**   b. **Juan**   c. **Pedro**

6. Estaba pensando para mis adentros que podría pedirle que se fuera en el _____ .
    a. **actor**   b. **acto**   c. **párrafo**

7. ¡Tengo los nervios de _____ !
    a. **pena**   b. **punto**   c. **punta**

8. Ayer hizo _____ mi florero favorito.
    a. **ánimos**   b. **añicos**   c. **años**

9. Estoy _____ de él.
    a. **harto**   b. **alto**   c. **acto**

10. Tengo ganas de romperle la _____ .
    a. **crisma**   b. **crisis**   c. **crismas**

C. Underline the correct definition for the expressions below.

1. **¡Dios me libre!:**
   a. Go with God!
        b. God forbid!

2. **no dar el brazo a torcer:**
   a. to eat like a pig
        b. to stick to one's guns

3. **largarse:**
   a. to arrive
        b. to leave

4. **pegársele como una ladilla:**
   a. to stick to someone like glue
        b. to be fed up

5. **no ser cosa de juego:**
   a. to get rid of
        b. to be no laughing matter

6. **deshacerse de:**
   a. to get rid of
        b. to manage to

7. **estar a dos dedos de:**
   a. to ignore
        b. to be on the verge of

8. **meterse en buen lío:**
   a. to have a falling out
        b. to get oneself into a mess

9. **en el acto:**
   a. immediately
        b. slowly

10. **partirle el corazón a uno:**
    a. to break someone's heart
         b. to ignore

11. **meter las narices en lo que a uno no le importa:**
    a. to butt into other people's business   b. to be on the verge of

12. **comer como un desfondado:**
    a. to eat like a bird
         b. to eat like a pig

LESSON EIGHT

El picnic
(The Picnic)

La última vez que yo vine aquí, miré con el rabo del ojo y vi a un tipo. ¡Después pasó corriendo a toda prisa y me di cuenta que estaba en cueros!

El tipo tenía que estar loco de remate.

EL PICNIC...

DIÁLOGO

Juan le convence a Teresa para **que vaya de picnic**.

Juan: **Me crujen las tripas**. Vamos a un restaurante.

Teresa: ¿Por qué malgastar nuestra **lana**? Se me ocurre algo. Hay un parque **a dos pasos de aquí**. Me estoy **muriendo de ganas** por ir de picnic y después **dar una vuelta** por el parque. Me encanta hacer eso en mis **ratos libres**. **De todas maneras**, es divertido **clavarle los ojos en** toda la gente.

Juan: Sería **padre tomar un poco de aire fresco**. ¡**O.K**, vámonos!

(Por fin)

Juan: No hay **ni cuatro gatos aquí**. Nunca se me olvidará lo que me pasó la última vez que estuve en este parque. Tenía los **huesos molidos** y me **dormí a fondo boca abajo**. Cuando me desperté, me di cuenta que había estado **lloviendo a cántaros** por una hora. ¡Estaba **hecho una sopa**! Y se me puso la **carne de gallina**.

Teresa: La última vez que yo vine aquí, miré con **el rabo del ojo** y vi a un tipo. ¡Después pasó corriendo **a toda prisa** y me di cuenta que estaba **en cueros**! **Se me pusieron los pelos de punta**.

Juan: El tipo tenía que estar **loco de remate**. ¡Me imagino que **hizo furor** con las mujeres!

Teresa: Bueno, a mí los **viejos verdes** me **revuelven las tripas**. ¡De todos modos, hay que estar **a la mira**!

THE PICNIC...

DIALOGUE

Juan convinces Teresa to go on a picnic.

Juan: I'm starving. Let's go to a restaurant.

Teresa: Why waste our money? I have an idea. There's a park that's a hop, skip and a jump from here. I'm dying to go on a picnic and then take a stroll through the park. I love doing that in my spare time. At any rate, it's fun to stare at all the people.

Juan: It would be nice to get a breath of fresh air. Okay, let's go!

(At last)

Juan: There's hardly a soul here. I'll never forget what happend to me last time I was at this park. I was wiped out and fell fast asleep lying on my stomach. When I woke up, I realized that it'd been raining like crazy for an hour. I was soaked! I got goose bumps.

Teresa: Last time I was here, I looked out of the corner of my eye and saw a guy. Then, he ran past at full speed and I noticed he was stark-naked! My hair stood on end.

Juan: The guy must have been nuts. I imagine he was quite a hit with the ladies!

Teresa: Well, dirty old men make my stomach turn. Anyway, we have to be on the lookout!

Literal Translation of Dialogue

DIALOGUE

Juan convinces Teresa to go on a picnic.

Juan: My intestines are growling. Let's go to a restaurant.

Teresa: Why waste our wool? Something occurs to me. There's a park two steps from here. I'm dying to go on a picnic and then give a turn through the park. It enchants me to do that in my free moments. In all manners, it's fun to nail the eyes at all the people.

Juan: It would be father to take some fresh air. O.K! Let's go.

             (For end)

Juan: There aren't even four cats here. I'll never forget what happened to me last time I was in this park. I had soft bones and fell asleep to the bottom mouth down. When I woke up, I realized it had been raining pitcherfuls for an hour. I was made a soup! I got chicken skin.

Teresa: The last time I came here, I saw a guy with the tail of the eye. Then, he ran by at all speed and I realized that he was in his own hide! My hair stood on end.

Juan: The guy must have been crazy to the end. I imagine that he made fury with the women.

Teresa: Well, green men make my guts turn. Anyway, we have to be on the look!

VOCABULARY

a dos pasos de aquí *exp.* a few steps away, a short distance from here, nearby
• (lit); two steps from here.

a fondo *exp.* completely, thoroughly • (lit); to the bottom • *dormir a fondo;* to
sleep deeply.
ALSO (1): **de fondo** *exp.* long-distance • (lit); of bottom • *corredor de fondo;*
long-distance runner.
ALSO (2): **en el fondo** *exp.* deep down (within a person) • *En el fondo, es muy
generoso;* Deep down, he's very generous.

a toda prisa *exp.* at full speed, as quickly as possible • (lit); at all speed.
SYNONYM (1): **a toda vela** *exp.* under full sail, at full speed • (lit); at all sail.
SYNONYM (2): **en un avemaría** *exp.* in a jiffy • (lit); in one Hail Mary.
SYNONYM (3): **en un chiflido** *exp.* in a jiffy • (lit); in one whistle.
SYNONYM (4): **en un credo** *exp.* in a jiffy • (lit); in one creed.
SYNONYM (5): **en un decir Jesús** *exp.* in a jiffy• (lit); in one saying of Jesus.
SYNONYM (6): **en un dos por tres** *exp.* in a jiffy • (lit); in a two by three.
SYNONYM (7): **en un improviso** *exp.* (Colombia, Venezuela, Mexico) in a jiffy
• (lit); in one sudden action.
SYNONYM (8): **en un salto** *exp.* in a jiffy • (lit); in one leap.
SYNONYM (9): **en un soplo** *exp.* in a jiffy • (lit); in a gust or blow.

boca abajo *exp.* face down • (lit); mouth down.
ANTONYM: **boca arriba** *exp.* face up • (lit); mouth up.

clavar los ojos en *exp.*: to stare at, to fix one's eyes on • (lit); to nail one's eyes
on.
SYNONYM (1): **clavar la vista en** *exp.* • (lit); to nail the sight on.
SYNONYM (2): **clavar la atención en** *exp.* • (lit); to fix one's attention on.
SYNONYM (3): **guiñar un ojo** *exp.* to make eyes at, to flirt • (lit); to wink (an
eye).
SYNONYM (4): **hacer ojos** *exp.* (Colombia) • (lit); to make eyes.
SYNONYM (5): **hacer ojitos** *exp.* (Mexico) • (lit); to make little eyes.
SYNONYM (6): **hacer caras** *exp.* (Eastern Argentina, Uruguay) • (lit); to make
faces.

crujirle las tripas *exp.* to be hungry (lit); to have one's intestines growl.
SYNONYM (1): **estar muriendo de hambre** *exp.* • (lit); to be dying of hunger.
SYNONYM (2): **comerse los puños** *exp.* to be famished • (lit); to eat one's fists.

cuatro gatos *exp.* hardly a soul, hardly anybody • (lit); four cats.
    ANTONYM: **más de cuatro** *exp.* many people.

dar una vuelta *exp.* to take a walk, a stroll • (lit); to give a turn.
    SYNONYM (1): **dar un paseo** *exp.* • (lit); to give a passage.
    SYNONYM (2): **pasear a pie** *exp.* • (lit); to walk by foot.

de todas maneras *exp.* at any rate, in any case, anyway • (lit); in all manners.
    SYNONYM: **de todos modos** *exp.* • (lit); in all modes.

en cueros *exp.* naked, in one's birthday suit • (lit); in (one's own) hide.
    SYNONYM (1): **en traje de Adán** *exp.* • (lit); in the suit of Adam.
    SYNONYM (2): **en pelota** *exp.* • (lit); in balls.
    SYNONYM (3): **pila** *f.* (Ecuador, Peru, Bolivia) • (lit); heap, pile.
    ALSO (1): **encuerado(a)** *adj.* • (lit); skinned.
    ALSO (2): **en cueros vivos** *exp.* stark-naked • (lit); in (one's own) living hide.

estar a la mira *exp.* to be on the lookout • (lit); to be on the look.
    NOTE: This comes from the verb *mirar* meaning "to look."
    SYNONYM: **estar truchas** *exp.* • (lit); to be trouts (because of their large wide open eyes).

estar hecho(a) una sopa *exp.* to be drenched • (lit); to be made into a soup.
    ALSO: **comer de la sopa boba** *exp.* to live off others.

estar loco(a) de remate *exp.* to be stark-raving mad, to be nuts • (lit); to be crazy to the end.
    ALSO (1): **como remate** *exp.* to top it off • *Y como remate perdí mis libros;* And to top it off, I lost my books.
    ALSO (2): **para remate** *exp.* to crown it all, on top of all that • (lit); to end.
    ALSO (3): **por remate** *exp.* finally, in the end, as a finishing touch • (lit); by end.

estar muriéndose de ganas por *exp.* to be dying to do something • (lit); to be dying with desire to.
    SYNONYM (1): **estar frito por hacer algo** *exp.* • (lit); to be fried to do something (English equivalent: "to be burning to do something").
    SYNONYM (2): **comerse de envidia por hacer algo** *exp.* • (lit); to eat oneself up with desire to do something.
    SYNONYM (3): **estar en plan de** *exp.* • (lit); to be in the scheme of [or] to have the mind set to.

hacer furor *exp.* to be a big event, to make a big splash • (lit); to make fury.
    SYNONYM: **tener un éxito padre** *exp.* to be a huge success • (lit); to have a huge success • SEE: **padre**.

ir de picnic *m.* to go on a picnic.
NOTE: This term has been borrowed from English and has become a popular replacement for the standard expression for "picnic," *día de campo.*

lana *f.* money, "dough" • (lit); wool.
SYNONYM: **pasta** *f.* (Spain)

llover a cántaros *exp.* to rain cats and dogs • (lit); to rain pitcherfuls.
SYNONYM (1): **llover a chorros** *exp.* • (lit); to rain in spurts.
SYNONYM (2): **llover con rabia** *exp.* (Cuba, Puerto Rico, Dominican Republic) • (lit); to rain with anger (or fury).
SYNONYM (3): **caer burros aparejados** *exp.* (Cuba, Puerto Rico, Dominican Republic) • (lit); to fall prepared donkeys.

mirar con el rabo del ojo *exp.* to look out of the corner of one's eye • (lit); to look out with the tail of the eye • *Me miró con el rabo del ojo;* He/She looked at me out of the corner of his/her eye.

O.K. *interj.* (Americanism) okay.
NOTE: This interjection has been borrowed from English and is becoming increasingly popular throughout the Spanish-speaking countries.
SYNONYM: **vale** *interj.* (Spain) • ¡*Vale!*; Okay! • (lit); worth • NOTE: This comes from the verb *valer* meaning "to be worth." • ALSO: **¡Sí, vale!** *interj.* Why, yes!

padre *adj.* (Mexico) **1.** nice, pleasant, enjoyable • **2.** huge • (lit); father.

ponérsele a uno la carne de gallina *exp.* to get goose bumps • (lit); to have one's flesh turn into that of a hen • *Me pone la carne de gallina;* It gives me goose bumps.
ALSO: **gallina** *m. & f.* coward, "chicken" • (lit); "chicken" • *Es una gallina;* He's/She's a coward.

ponérsele los pelos de punta *exp.* to have one's hair stand on end • (lit); to put one's hairs on end.
ALSO: **cortar/partir un cabello en el aire** *exp.* to split hairs • (lit); to cut/to split a hair in the air.

por fin *exp.* at last, finally • (lit); to the end • *Al fin llegó;* At last, he/she showed up.

ratos libres *exp.* in spare time, in leisure hours • (lit); free moments.
SYNONYM: **a ratos perdidos** *exp.* in lost moments.

revolverle las tripas *exp.* to turn one's stomach • (lit); to stir one's guts.
SYNONYM: **revolverle el estómago** *exp.* • (lit); to stir one's stomach.

tener los huesos molidos *exp.* to be wiped-out, exhausted, ready to collapse •
(lit); to have ground-up bones.
SYNONYM: **estar hecho un trapo** *exp.* to be made a rag.

tomar un poco de aire fresco *adj.* to get some fresh air • (lit); to take a little of
the fresh air.
SYNONYM: **tomar el fresco** *exp.* • (lit); to take some fresh (air).
ALSO: **ponerse fresco** *exp.* to put on light clothing (for the summer, etc.) •
(lit); to put oneself fresh.

viejo verde *exp.* dirty old man • (lit); a green man.
NOTE: In Spanish, when the color *verde* meaning "green" is used as an
adjective, it has the connotation of "dirty, lewd, or sexual." In English, the
color "blue" has this distinction.
SYNONYM: **viejo rabo verde** *exp.* • (lit); old green tail.
ALSO: **un chiste verde** *exp.* a dirty joke • (lit); a green joke • ALSO: **un chiste
rojo** *exp.* a dirty joke • NOTE: The adjective *rojo,* meaning "red," also has the
connotation of "dirty, lewd, or sexual."

PRACTICE THE VOCABULARY

[Answers to Lesson 8, p. 121]

A. Complete the sentences by choosing the correct word(s) from the list below.

tripas	de remate	fondo
molidos	pasos	muriendo
de punta	clavarle los ojos	cántaros
ratos	fresco	gatos
mira	en cueros	furor

1. Me gustaría tomar un poco de aire _____ .

2. El tipo tenía que estar loco _____ .

3. Tengo los huesos _____ .

4. Dormí a _____ boca abajo.

5. Me gusta leer en mis _____ libres.

6. Es divertido _____ en toda la gente.

7. Está lloviendo a _____ ahora.

8. No hay ni cuatro _____ aquí.

9. Hay un parque a dos _____ de aquí.

10. Me crujen las _____ .

11. Me estoy _____ de ganas por ir de picnic.

12. Se me pusieron los cabellos _____ .

13. De todos modos, hay que estar a la _____ .

14. No tenía nada puesto. Estaba _____ .

15. El espectáculo hizo _____ .

B. Underline the word(s) in parentheses that best complete(s) the sentence.

1. El pobrecito no tiene (**lana, lama, laja**).

2. A mí los viejos (**verdes, amarillos, blancos**) me revuelven (**los brazos, los ojos, las tripas**).

3. De (**algunas, toros, todas**) maneras, no me gusta.

4. Se me pusieron los (**rabos, huesos, pelos**).

5. La última vez que yo vine aquí, miré a un tipo con el (**rabino, rabo, rabinato**) del ojo.

6. Después de la cena, me gustaría dar (**una vuelta, uno vuelto, un vuelco**) por el parque.

7. No hay ni (**dos, tres, cuatro**) gatos aquí.

8. Me voy a acostar. Tengo los huesos (**molidos, duros, fracturados**).

9. Sería (**madre, hermana, padre**) ir al cine esta noche.

10. Anoche, dormí a (**fondo, fonda, fon**).

11. Me crujen (**los brazos, los ojos, las tripas**).

12. Hay que estar a la (**mar, madre, mira**).

C. Circle the words in the grid on page 95 that fit the expressions below. Words may be spelled in any direction, even backwards or upside down! The first one has been done for you.

1. **ponérsele los** _____*pelos*_____ **de punta** *exp.* to have one's hair stand on end

2. **estar hecho una** _____ *exp.* to be drenched

3. **viejo** _____ *exp.* dirty old man

4. **llover a** _____ *exp.* to rain cats and dogs

5. **mirar con el** _____ **del ojo** *exp.* to look out of the corner of one's eye

6. **dar una** _____ *exp.* to take a walk, a stroll

7. **tener los huesos** _____ *exp.* to be wiped out, exhausted

8. **revolverle las** _____ *exp.* to turn one's stomach

9. **ponérsele a uno la** _____ **de gallina** *exp.* to get goose bumps

10. **ni** _____ *exp.* hardly a soul, hardly anybody

11. _____ *exp.* face down

12. **dos** _____ **de aquí** *exp.* nearby

13. **en** _____ *exp.* naked, in one's birthday suit

14. **hacer** _____ *exp.* to be a big event, to make a big splash

WORD GAME FOR EXERCISE C

C	Á	N	T	A	R	O	S	G	L	S	O
F	U	S	D	E	U	F	U	R	O	R	Q
T	S	A	P	A	T	S	P	D	P	X	Z
B	O	B	T	E	O	S	I	V	A	H	A
C	R	M	N	R	M	L	E	E	S	T	C
S	I	A	E	B	O	F	V	R	O	R	A
O	J	U	D	M	M	G	E	D	S	I	R
L	C	V	U	E	L	T	A	E	F	P	N
E	N	M	O	M	H	S	D	T	I	A	E
P	R	A	B	O	L	O	E	M	O	S	L
N	A	N	C	E	I	P	D	O	M	S	T
O	L	O	J	A	B	A	A	C	O	B	L

D. Match the Spanish with the English.

☐ 1. I'm starving.

☐ 2. I imagine he was quite a hit with the ladies.

☐ 3. I realized he was stark-naked.

☐ 4. I was soaked.

☐ 5. I had goose bumps for a week.

☐ 6. He was lying face down.

☐ 7. I want to get some fresh air.

☐ 8. Okay, let's go.

☐ 9. It's fun to gawk at all the people.

☐ 10. There's a park that's real close to here.

☐ 11. At last, he arrived.

☐ 12. It would be neat to see her again.

A. **Sería padre verla otra vez.**

B. **Tenía la carne de gallina por una semana.**

C. **Me crujen las tripas.**

D. **Por fin, llegó.**

E. **Estaba hecho una sopa.**

F. **O.K., vámonos.**

G. **Me di cuenta que estaba en cueros.**

H. **Hay un parque a dos pasos de aquí.**

I. **Me imagino que hizo furor con las mujeres.**

J. **Es divertido clavarle los ojos en toda la gente.**

K. **Quiero tomar un poco de aire fresco.**

L. **Estaba tumbado boca abajo.**

LESSON NINE

Por teléfono

(On the Telephone)

"Ya ve al grano!
Dime... ¿qué pasó?"

"No digas ni pío acerca de esto,
pero acabo de enterar me que
Juan rompió con Nina!"

Lección nueve

POR TELÉFONO...

DIÁLOGO

Gina y Laura están hablando por teléfono.

Gina: Siempre te **andas por las ramas**. Ya ve **al grano**. Dime... ¿qué pasó?

Laura: **No digas ni pío** acerca de esto, pero **acabo de** enterar me que Juan **rompió con** Nina.

Gina: Debe de haber estado **al borde del** llanto.

Laura: ¡Sencillamente **rompió a** llorar! ¡Pero **lágrimas de cocodrilo**!

Gina: No te quiero **cortar el hilo** pero si me pasara a mí, me darían deseos de **saltarme la tapa de los sesos**.

Laura: La dejó **sin más ni más**. ¡A que ya estaba saliendo con otra **a espaldas** de ella! **Desde luego**, **a la corta o a la larga**, **cantará de plano** y se lo dirá **cara a cara**.

Gina: Tú sabes que él siempre ha tenido novias **sin número**. **Bueno, tarde o temprano** iba a pasar.

Laura: ¡**Qué** muchas novias **ni qué ocho cuartos**! Eso es lo que le cuenta a todo el mundo.

Gina: **¿A santo de qué?**

Laura: Le gusta jactarse. ¡Una noche simplemente la **dejó plantada**! **No hay pero que valga**. Nunca ha tratado bien a las mujeres y sé de quien lo heredó; **de tal palo, tal astilla**. Por eso es que su padre y él son **uña y carne**.

Gina: Bueno, **Dios los cría y ellos se juntan**.

Laura: Nadie me ha pedido mi opinión, pero me parece muy bien que se haya librado de él **de una vez y para siempre**.

ON THE TELEPHONE...

DIALOGUE

Gina and Laura are talking on the phone.

Gina: You always beat around the bush. Just get to the point. Tell me… what happened?

Laura: Don't breathe a word about it, but I just heard that Juan broke up with Nina.

Gina: She must have been on the verge of tears.

Laura: She just burst out crying! I mean crocodile tears!

Gina: I don't mean to interrupt, but if that had happened to me, I'd feel like blowing my brains out!

Laura: He left her just like that. I bet he was already going out with someone behind her back! Of course, eventually, he'll confess and tell her face to face.

Gina: You know, he's always had countless girl friends. Well, I knew it would happen sooner or later.

Laura: A lot of girl friends, my eye! He tells everyone that.

Gina: What the heck for?

Laura: He just likes to brag. He just stood her up one night! No buts about it. He's never been nice to women and I know where he gets it from; like father like son. That's why he and his father are so close.

Gina: Well, birds of a feather flock together.

Laura: No one asked my opinion, but I think it's a good thing that she's rid of him once and for all.

Literal Translation of Dialogue

DIALOGUE

Gina and Laura are talking on the phone.

Gina:	You always walk by the branches. Just get to the seed. Tell me... what happened?
Laura:	Don't say a chirp about this, but I just finished hearing that Juan broke with Nina.
Gina:	I'm sure she was at the edge of tears.
Laura:	She simply broke out in crying! But crocodile tears!
Gina:	I don't want to cut your thread, but if that had happened to me, I'd feel like blowing up the lid of my brains.
Laura:	He left her without anything further or anything more. I bet he was already going out with someone else at the back of her. Since then, in the short or in the long, he'll eventually sing straightforwardly and tell her face to face.
Gina:	You know that he's always had girl friends without number. Good, late or early it would happen.
Laura:	(SEE: Vocabulary **¡qué... ni qué ocho cuartos!**) He tells everyone that.
Gina:	To saint of what?
Laura:	He just likes to brag. One night he simply left her planted! There is no but that is worthwhile. He's never treated women well and I know from whom he inherits it; from such a stick, such a splinter. That's why he and his father are fingernail and flesh.
Gina:	Good, God raises them and they get together.
Laura:	Nobody has asked me my opinion, but it seems to me that it's a good thing that she's free of him for one time and for always.

VOCABULARY

a espaldas de alguien *exp.* behind someone's back • (lit); to the back of someone.
ALSO (1): **echarse algo sobre las espaldas** *exp.* to bear a burden • (lit); to throw something on one's back.
ALSO (2): **tirar de espaldas a alguien** *exp.* to floor someone (with news) • (lit); to throw someone on his/her back • *Esta noticia me tiró de espaldas;* This piece of news just floored me.

a la corta o a la larga *exp.* in the short or long run • (lit); in the short (run) or in the long (run).
SYNONYM: **a la larga** *exp.* in the long run • (lit); in the long.

a santo de qué *exp.* for what reason • (lit); to saint of what.
ALSO (1): **santo(a)** *adj.* blessed • (lit); holy • *Todo el santo día;* The whole blessed day.
ALSO (2): **desnudar a un santo para vestir a otro** *exp.* to rob Peter to pay Paul • (lit); to undress a saint to clothe another.

acabar de (+ infinitive) *exp.* to have just (+ past participle) • (lit); to finish.
SYNONYM (1): **venir de (+ infinitive)** *exp.* (Colombia) • (lit); to come to (+ infinitive).
SYNONYM (2): **recién (+ past participle)** *exp.* (Eastern Argentina, Uruguay, Chile) • (lit); recent (+ past participle).

andarse por las ramas *exp.* to beat around the bush • (lit); to stroll/walk by the branches.
SYNONYM: **andar con rodeos** *exp.* • (lit); to walk with detours.
NOTE: **emborrachar la perdiz** *exp.* (Chile) to beat around the bush • (lit); to get the partridge drunk.

bueno(a) *adj. & interj.* **1.** well… • **2.** fine! • **3.** bad, nasty • *un buen constipado;* a nasty cold • **4.** considerable • *una buena cantidad;* a considerable amount • **5.** come off it! • **6.** okay.

cantar de plano *exp.* to make a full confession, to confess, to spill the beans • (lit); to sing straightforwardly.
NOTE: **de plano** *exp.* directly, straightforwardly.

cara a cara *exp.* **1.** right to a person's face • **2.** privately • (lit); face to face.
ALSO (1): **tener mucha cara** *exp.* to have a lot of nerve • (lit); to have a lot of face • *Ese tipo tiene mucha cara;* That guy's got a lot of nerve • *No tengo cara para hacer algo;* I don't have the nerve to do that.
ALSO (2): **dar la cara** *exp.* to face up to things • (lit); to give face.
ALSO (3): **dar/sacar la cara por uno** *exp.* to stand up for someone, to defend

someone • (lit); to give/to stick out the face for someone.

ALSO (4): **poner a mal tiempo buena cara** *exp.*to keep a stiff upper lip • (lit); to put good face in bad times.

ALSO (5): **poner buena cara a algo** *exp.*to take something well • (lit); to put good face to something.

ALSO (6): **tener cara de** *exp.* to look • (lit); to have face of • *Tener cara de tristeza;* To look sad.

cortarle el hilo a alguien *exp.* to interrupt someone • (lit); to cut the thread of someone.

SYNONYM: **cortarle el hilo/la hebra a alguien** *exp.* • (lit); to cut the thread/filament of someone.

ALSO: **perder el hilo/la hebra de** *exp.* to lose the thread/filament of (a conversation, etc.)

de tal palo, tal astilla *exp.* like father, like son • (lit); from such a stick, such a splinter.

SYNONYM (1): **de casta le viene al galgo ser rabilargo** *exp.* like father, like son • (lit); from the breed the greyhound gets to be long-tailed.

SYNONYM (2): **cual el cuervo, tal su huevo** *exp.* • (lit); like the raven, like the egg.

SYNONYM (3): **de tal jarro, tal tepalcate** *exp.* (Mexico).

de una vez y para siempre *exp.* once and for all • (lit); for one time and for always.

SYNONYM: **de una vez** *exp.* • (lit); for one time.

dejar alguien plantado(a) *exp.* **1.** to stand someone up • (lit); to leave someone planted • **2.** to leave someone in the lurch, to walk out on someone.

ALSO: **bien plantado(a)** *adj.* handsome, well-turned out • (lit); well-planted.

SYNONYM (1): **dejar en las astas del toro** *exp.* • (lit); to leave in the spears of the bull.

SYNONYM (2): **dejar a uno embarcado** *exp.* (Mexico) • (lit); to leave someone embarked.

desde luego *exp.* certainly, of course • (lit); since then.

SYNONYM: **por supuesto** *exp.* of course, certainly • (lit); for supposed.

Dios los cría y ellos se juntan *exp.* birds of a feather flock together • (lit); God raises them and they get together.

estar al borde del llanto *exp.* to be on the verge of tears • (lit); to be on the edge of weeping.

ir al grano *exp.* to get to the point • (lit); to go to the seed.

NOTE: This could best be compared to the American expression, "to get to the heart of the matter."

SYNONYM: **llegar al caso** *exp.* • (lit); to arrive to the case.

lágrimas de cocodrilo *exp.* • (lit); crocodile tears.
> ALSO (1): **beberse/tragarse las lágrimas** *exp.* to hold back one's tears • (lit); to drink/to swallow one's tears.
> ALSO (2): **ser el paño de lágrimas de alguien** *exp.* to give someone a shoulder to cry on • (lit); to be someone's tear cloth.

no decir ni pío *exp.* not to say a word, not to say a peep • (lit); not to say a chirp.
> ALSO: **pío** *m.* desire, yearning • (lit); chirping, clucking.

¡No hay pero que valga! *exp.* no buts about it! • (lit); there is no but that is worthwhile.
> NOTE: This expression can also be used in the plural: *¡No hay peros que valgan!*

¡qué... ni qué ocho cuartos! *exp.* my foot!
> NOTE: When this expression surrounds a noun, such as *¡Qué **novias** ni qué ocho cuartos!* the free translation becomes "Girl friends, my eye!" • This expression does not lend itself to a literal translation.

romper a *exp.* to begin to, to burst out, to suddenly start to • (lit); to break (out) to.
> SYNONYM: **deshacerse en** *v.* • (lit); to undo oneself in.

romper con *exp.* to break up with • (lit); to break with.
> SYNONYM: **tronar con** *v.* to break off relations with • (lit); to thunder.

saltarse la tapa de los sesos *exp.* to blow one's brains out • (lit); to blow up the lid of the brains.
> ALSO: **perder el seso** *exp.* to lose one's head, to go out of one's mind • (lit); to lose the brain.

ser uña y carne *exp.* to be inseparable, to be hand in glove • (lit); to be fingernail and flesh.
> ALSO: **esconder las uñas** *exp.* to hide one's true intentions • (lit); to hide the fingernails • ANTONYM: **sacar las uñas** *exp.* to show one's true colors.

sin más ni más *exp.* just like that • (lit); without anything further or anything more.

sin número *exp.* countless • (lit); without number.
> ALSO: **número** *m.* performance (of a cabaret, circus, etc.).

tarde o temprano *exp.* sooner or later, eventually • (lit); late or early.
> ALSO: **más tarde o más temprano** *exp.* • (lit); later or earlier.

PRACTICE THE VOCABULARY

[Answers to Lesson 9, p. 123]

A. Choose the expression in the second column that matches the definition on the left.

1. _____ *exp.* to beat around the bush

2. _____ *exp.* in the long run

3. _____ *exp.* like father, like son

4. _____ *exp.* not to say a word

5. _____ *exp.* to begin to, to burst out, to suddenly start to

6. _____ *exp.* to interrupt someone

7. _____ *exp.* to get to the point

8. _____ *exp.* to be inseparable

9. _____ *exp.* to break up with

10. _____ *exp.* countless

11. _____ *exp.* to blow one's brains out

12. _____ *exp.* to make a full confession

13. _____ *exp.* no buts about it

14. _____ *exp.* sooner or later

A. **sin número**

B. **de tal palo, tal astilla**

C. **andarse por las ramas**

D. **cantar de plano**

E. **a la corta o a la larga**

F. **ir al grano**

G. **ser uña y carne**

H. **saltarse la tapa de los sesos**

I. **ortarle el hilo a alguien**

J. **no decir ni pío**

K. **romper a**

L. **romper con**

M. **tarde o temprano**

N. **no hay pero que valga**

B. Underline the word(s) in parentheses that best complete(s) the sentence.

1. ¿Qué pasó? Ya ve al (**grado, gratín, grano**).

2. No digas ni (**pica, pie, pío**).

3. Se libró de él de una (**vez, vaso, vía**) y para siempre.

4. De tal (**palco, pan, palo**), tal astilla.

5. Tú sabes que él siempre ha tenido novias sin (**letra, color, número**).

6. Rompió con ella sin más ni (**más, poco, bastante**).

7. ¡Sencillamente (**rompió, tropecé, cantó**) a llorar!

8. Seguro que estaba al (**borde, bordo, bordón**) del llanto.

9. ¿A (**dios, santo, ángel**) de qué?

10. Tarde o (**templado, temporada, temprano**) iba a pasar.

11. No hay (**pero, y, o**) que valga.

12. Su padre y él son uña y (**pie, carne, brazo**).

13. A la corta o a la (**lanza, lanzada, larga**), es mejor.

14. Cantará de (**piano, plano, plantado**).

C. Match the English with the Spanish.

☐ 1. You know, he's always had countless girl friends.

☐ 2. He confessed and told her to her face.

☐ 3. Like father, like son.

☐ 4. Don't breathe a word about it.

☐ 5. I don't mean to interrupt but I don't agree.

☐ 6. I just found out.

☐ 7. You always beat around the bush.

☐ 8. Birds of a feather flock together.

☐ 9. If that had happened to me, I'd blow my brains out.

☐ 10. He broke up with her ust like that.

A. **Siempre te andas por las ramas.**

B. **¿A santo de qué?**

C. **Dios los cría y ellos se juntan.**

D. **Tú sabes que él siempre ha tenido novias sin número.**

E. **Acabo de enterarme.**

F. **Bueno, tarde o temprano iba a pasar.**

G. **No te quiero cortar el hilo pero no estoy de acuerdo.**

H. **Si me pasara a mí, me darían deseos de saltarme la tapa de los sesos.**

I. **De tal palo, tal astilla.**

J. **¡Qué fantasmas ni qué ocho cuartos!**

☐ 11. Well, it was going to happen sooner or later.

☐ 12. What in the world for?

☐ 13. I bet he was going out with someone else behind her back.

☐ 14. Ghosts, my eye!

K. **A que ya estaba saliendo con otra a espaldas de ella.**

L. **Rompió con ella sin más ni más.**

M. **Cantó de plano y se lo dijo cara a cara.**

N. **No digas ni pío acerca de esto.**

D. Step 1: Complete the following expressions by choosing the appropriate words from the list below. Make sure to write your answers in the boxes provided.

Step 2: Transfer the letters in the bold boxes in order of appearance to the crossword grid on page 108 to reveal a popular Spanish expression which means, "to talk nonstop."

WORD LIST

ROMPER	SIN	HILO
LUEGO	LARGA	PALO
ESPALDAS	RAMAS	SIEMPRE
CANTAR	PLANTADO	

1. like father, like son

D	E		T	A	L	■				■	T	A	L
A	S	T	I	L	L	A							

2. to interrupt someone

C	O	R	T	A	R	L	E	·	E	L	■				
A	■	A	L	G	U	I	E	N							

3. to beat around the bush

| A | N | D | A | R | S | E | | P | O | R | | L | A | S |

4. in the long run

| A | | L | A | | C | O | R | T | A | | O |
| A | | L | A | | | | | | | | |

5. **1.** to stand someone up • **2.** to leave someone in the lurch

| D | E | J | A | R | | A | L | G | U | I | E | N |
| | | | | | | | | | | | | |

6. once and for all

| D | E | | U | N | A | | V | E | Z | | Y |
| P | A | R | A | | | | | | | | |

7. to make a full confession, to spill the beans

| | | | | | | D | E | | P | L | A | N | O |

8. to begin to, to burst out

| | | | | | | A |

9. behind someone's back

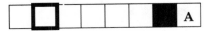

| A | | | | | | | | | D | E |
| A | L | G | U | I | E | N | | | | |

10. certainly, of course

| D | E | S | D | E | ■ | | | | □ |

11. countless

| □ | | ■ | N | Ú | M | E | R | O |

"To talk nonstop"

De viaje

(On a Trip)

Vamos, ponme al corriente.
¿Qué tal las vacaciones con Ramón?

Lección diez

DE VIAJE...

DIÁLOGO

Eduardo le está contando a León acerca de su viaje.

León: Vamos, ponme **al corriente**. ¿Qué tal las vacaciones con Ramón?

Eduardo: Fue horrible **de cabo a rabo**. Siempre pensé que sería divertido **ir de vacaciones** con él pero **el hábito no hace al monje. Por una parte** es **buena gente y por otra** me **vuelve loco**. Es que me **saca de quicio**. Estuve **al punto** de **hacer el equipaje** y regresar a casa al día siguiente... o de **mandarlo a bañar**. Pensé que íbamos a **ir a medias** en todo pero no logré que **aflojara pasta**. Ahora, ¡**no tengo dónde caerme muerto**!

León: ¿**De veras**?

Eduardo: Fue **la gota que derramó el vaso**. A **llamar al pan pan y al vino vino**. El tipo es tacaño.

León: Me sorprende que no te hayas **echado atrás** sabiendo como es él. **Por lo visto**, no lo pasaste nada bien.

Eduardo: **En resumidas cuentas**, no volveré a **tener nada que ver con** él.

León: Bueno, creo que pronto **harán las paces**.

Eduardo: Es que tenía tantas ganas de **hacer puente** y relajarme. Ahora **no puedo más**.

Lesson Ten

ON A TRIP...

DIALOGUE

Eduardo is telling León about his trip.

_____

León:	So bring me up-to-date. How was your vacation with Ramón?
Eduardo:	It was terrible from beginning to end. I always thought it would be fun to go on vacation with him but you can't judge a book by its cover. On the one hand, he can be a nice guy, on the other hand, he drives me crazy. He just exasperates me. I was on the verge of packing my bags and coming home the next day... or telling him to take a flying leap! I thought we were going to go halves on everything but I couldn't get him to cough up any money. Now I'm flat broke!
León:	Really?
Eduardo:	That was the last straw. Let's call a spade a spade. The guy is stingy.
León:	I'm surprised you didn't back out knowing what he's like. Well, by the looks of it, you didn't have a good time at all.
Eduardo:	In short, I'll have nothing to do with him again.
León:	Well, I think you'll make up soon.
Eduardo:	It's just that I was so looking forward to taking a long weekend and relaxing. Now I'm exhausted.

Literal Translation of Dialogue

DIALOGUE

Eduardo is telling León about his trip.

León: So put me to the current. How was your trip with Ramón?

Eduardo: It was horrible from end to tail. I always thought it would be fun to go on vacation with him but clothes don't make the man. For one part, he is good people and for the other, he turns me crazy. He brings me out of my mental state. I was on the point of making my baggage and coming home the next day... or telling him to go take a bath! I thought we were going to go to halves on everything but I couldn't get him to loosen dough. Now I don't have a place to fall down dead.

León: From truth?

Eduardo: That was the drop that made the glass spill over. Let's call the bread, bread and the wine, wine. The guy is stingy.

León: I'm surprised you didn't throw yourself backwards knowing what he's like. By the sight, you didn't have anything of a good time.

Eduardo: In summarized calculations, I won't have anything to see with him.

León: Fine, I think that you'll make peace soon.

Eduardo: It's just that I was looking forward to making a bridge and relaxing. Now I'm unable to go on anymore.

VOCABULARY

aflojar *v.* (Mexico, Cuba, Puerto Rico, Dominican Republic, Eastern Argentina, Uruguay) to fork out, to cough up • (lit); to loosen.
SYNONYM: **soltar** *v.* • (lit); to release.

buena gente *exp.* good egg, nice guy • (lit); good people.

de cabo a rabo *exp.* from beginning to end • (lit); from end to tail.
SYNONYM (1): **de cabo a cabo** *exp.* • (lit); from end to end.
SYNONYM (2): **de punta a punta** *exp.* • (lit); from point to point.
ALSO: **no dejar cabo suelto** *exp.* not to leave any loose ends • (lit); not to leave loose end.

de veras *exp.* really, honestly, is that so • (lit); from truth.

echarse atrás *exp.* to back out • (lit); to throw oneself backwards
ALSO: **volverse/echarse para atrás** *exp.* to go back on one's word • (lit); to turn/to throw oneself backwards.

el hábito no hace al monje *exp.* you can't judge a book by it's cover • (lit); the habit doesn't make the monk.
SYNONYM: **caras vemos, corazones no sabemos** *exp.* • (lit); faces we see, hearts we don't know.

en resumidas cuentas *exp.* in brief, in short, getting to the bottom line • (lit); in summarized calculations.
SYNONYM (1): **en resumen** *exp.* • (lit); in summary.
SYNONYM (2): **en resolución** *exp.* • (lit); in resolution.
SYNONYM (3): **al fin y al cabo** *exp.* • (lit); to the end and the end.

estar a punto de *exp.* • (lit); to be on the point of • NOTE: This expression is always followed by a verb, i.e. *Estuve al punto de llorar;* I was on the verge of crying.
SYNONYM (1): **estar al borde de** *exp.* to be on the verge of, to be on the brink of • (lit); to be on the edge of • NOTE: This expression is always followed by a noun, i.e. *Estuve al borde del llanto;* I was on the brink of tears.
SYNONYM (2): **estar a dos dedos de** *exp.* • (lit); to be two fingers (away) from • NOTE: This expression is always followed by a verb, i.e. *Estuve a dos dedos de gritar;* I was on the verge of screaming.

hacer el equipaje *exp.* to pack one's bags • (lit); to do one's baggage.

hacer las paces *exp.* to make up after a quarrel • (lit); to make peace.
ANTONYM: **romper con** *exp.* to have a falling out • (lit); to break with.

hacer puente *exp.* to take a long weekend • (lit); to make a bridge (between Sunday and Monday).
ALSO: **puente** *m.* long weekend • (lit); bridge.

ir a medias *exp.* to go to halves, fifty-fifty • (lit); to go to the halves.
    SYNONYM (1): **ir a la mitad** *exp.* • (lit); to go to the half.
    SYNONYM (2): **ir mitad mitad** *exp.* • (lit); to go half-half.

ir de vacaciones *exp.* to go on vacation • (lit); to go of vacations.
    ALSO: **estar de vacaciones** *exp.* to be on vacation • (lit); to be of vacations.
    NOTE: The feminine noun *vacaciones* is always in the plural form.
    SYNONYM: **estar de viaje** *exp.* • (lit); to be of trip.

la gota que derrama el vaso *exp.* the last straw, the straw that broke the camel's back • (lit); the drop that makes the glass spill over.
    SYNONYM (1): **¡No faltaba más! / ¡Lo que faltaba! / ¡Sólo faltaba eso!** *exp.* That's the last straw! • (lit); Nothing else was missing! / What was missing! / Only that was missing!
    SYNONYM (2): **la última gota que hace rebasar la copa** *exp.* • (lit); the last drop that makes the glass overflow.
    SYNONYM (3): **es el colmo** *exp.* • (lit); it is the height (or: that's the limit).

llamar al pan pan y al vino vino *exp.* to call a spade a spade, to call it like it is • (lit); to call bread, bread and wine, wine.

mandar a alguien a bañar *exp.* • to tell someone to go take a flying leap! • (lit); to send someone to go take a bath • *¡Vete a bañar!;* Go fly a kite!
    NOTE: The following are other ways to say, "Go fly a kite!"
    (1): **¡Vete a ver si ya puso la cochina/puerca!** *exp.* • (lit); Go see if the sow has already laid an egg.
    (2): **¡Vete a echar pulgas a otra parte!** *exp.* • (lit); Go throw fleas somewhere else.
    (3): **¡Vete a freír espárragos!** *exp.* (lit); Go fry asparagus.
    (4): **¡Vete a freír chongos!** *exp.* (Mexico) • (lit); Go fry buns!
    (5): **¡Vete a freír monos!** *exp.* (Colombia) • (lit); Go fry monkeys!
    (6): **¡Vete a freír mocos!** *exp.* (Ecuador, Peru, Bolivia) • (lit); Go fry mucus!

no poder más *exp.* to be exhausted • (lit); to be unable to do anything more.
    SYNONYM (1): **tener los huesos molidos** *exp.* • (lit); to have one's bones ground up (or more literally, to be tired to the bone).
    SYNONYM (2): **estar molido(a)** *exp.* to be ground up or pulverized.
    SYNONYM (3): **estar muerto(a)** *exp.* • (lit); to be dead (tired).
    SYNONYM (4): **estar más muerto(a) que vivo(a)** *exp.* • (lit); to be more dead than alive.

no tener dónde caerse muerto *exp.* to be flat broke • (lit); not to have a place to fall down dead.

no tener nada que ver con *exp.* to have nothing to do with • (lit); to have nothing to see with.
    SYNONYM: **no tener arte ni parte en** *exp.* not to have art nor part with.

pasta *f.* (Spain) dough, cash, loot • (lit); paste, dough.
   ALSO: **tener pasta de** *exp.* to have the makings of • (lit); to have the paste of.

poner al corriente *exp.* to bring up-to-date, to inform, to give the lowdown •
   (lit); to put in the current or "in the flow of knowledge."
   SYNONYM: **poner al día** *exp.* • (lit); to put to the day.
   ALSO (1): **corriente** *f.* trend • *las últimas corrientes de la moda;* the latest fashion
   trends.
   ALSO (2): **llevarle/seguirle la corriente a uno** *exp.* to humor someone, to go
   right along with that which is being said • (lit); to carry / to follow the current
   to someone.

por lo visto *exp.* apparently, by the looks of, obviously • (lit); by what is seen.
   SYNONYM: **está visto que** *exp.* it's obvious that • (lit); it's seen that.

por una parte… y por otra *exp.* on the one hand… and the other • (lit); for one
   part and for another.
   ALSO: **de parte a parte** *exp.* back and forth, from one side to the other.
   SYNONYM: **por un lado… y por otro** *exp.* • (lit); for one side… and for the
   other.

sacar de quicio a uno *exp.* to exasperate or infuriate someone • (lit); to take
   someone out of a doorjamb.
   SYNONYM: **freír** *v.* • (lit); to fry.

volver loco a uno *exp.* to drive someone crazy • (lit); to turn someone crazy.
   ALSO: **loco(a)** *adj.* wonderful yet hard to believe • *Tener una suerte loca;* To
   have unbelievable luck.

PRACTICE THE VOCABULARY

[Answers to Lesson 10, p. 125]

A. Complete the sentences by choosing the appropriate words from the list below.

equipaje	corriente	punto
cuentas	ver	muerto
medias	rabo	gente
paces	puente	hábito

1. Ponme al _____ . ¿Qué pasó?

2. Tenía tantas ganas de hacer _____ y relajarme.

3. Fue horrible de cabo a ___ _____ .

4. Creo que pronto harán las _____ .

5. En resumidas _____ , no volveré a tener nada que
   _____ con él.

6. Ese tipo es buena _____ .

7. Pensé que íbamos a ir a _____ .

8. El _____ no hace al monje.

9. Ahora, ¡no tengo dónde caerme _____ !

10. Estuve al _____ de hacer el _____
    y regresar a casa.

B. Underline the correct translation.

1. **de cabo a rabo**:
   a. from beginnng to end   b. from top to bottom

2. **llamar al pan pan y al vino vino**:
   a. to call for room service   b. to call a spade a spade

3. **la gota que derramó el vaso**:
   a. the last straw   b. from beginning to end

4. **por lo visto**:
   a. by the sound of it   b. by the looks of it

5. **no poder más**:
   a. to be wide-awake   b. to be exhausted

6. **ir a medias**:
   a. to go halves   b. to travel halfway

7. **echarse atrás**:
   a. to look back   b. to back out

8. **volver loco**:
   a. to drive crazy   b. to drive crazily

9. **aflojar**:
   a. to hoard   b. to give

10. **hacer las paces**:
   a. to make up   b. to have a fight

11. **en resumidas cuentas**:
   a. to drag on   b. in short

12. **no tener dónde caerse muerto**:
   a. to be broke   b. to be rich

13. **hacer puente**:
   a. to burn one's bridges   b. to take a long weekend

14. **sacar de quicio**:
   a. to infuriate   b. to please

C. Match the English with the Spanish.

☐ 1. Bring me up-to-date.

☐ 2. That was the last straw.

☐ 3. I'm exhausted.

☐ 4. It was terrible from beginning to end.

☐ 5. You can't judge a book by its cover.

☐ 6. By the looks of it, you didn't have a good time at all.

☐ 7. On one hand, he is a nice guy.

☐ 8. He drives me crazy.

☐ 9. I was on the verge of telling him where to go.

☐ 10. I couldn't get him to cough up any money.

☐ 11. Really?

☐ 12. I'll have nothing to do with him again.

A. **No logré que aflojara pasta.**

B. **¿De veras?**

C. **Me vuelve loco.**

D. **Fue horrible de cabo a rabo.**

E. **No volveré a tener nada que ver con él.**

F. **No puedo más.**

G. **Ponme al corriente.**

H. **Por una parte es buena gente.**

I. **Fue la gota que derramó el vaso.**

J. **Por lo visto, no lo pasaste nada bien.**

K. **El hábito no hace al monje.**

L. **Estuve a punto de mandarlo a bañar.**

D. Step 1 • Each word in the following expressions have been scrambled. Write the unscrambled words in the boxes below. The first one has been done for you.

1. **ed boca a bora** *exp.* from beginning to end.

0	1		2	3	4	5		6		7	8	9	10
D	E	■	C	A	B	O	■	A	■	R	A	B	O

2. **pro lo sivot** *exp.* by the looks of it.

11	12	13		14	15		16	17	18	19	20
			■			■					

3. **¿ed sarev?** *exp.* really?

21	22		23	24	25	26	27
		■					

4. **herac neupte** *exp.* to take a long weekend.

28	29	30	31	32		33	34	35	36	37	38
					■						

5. **on derpo smá** *exp.* to be exhausted.

39	40		41	42	43	44	45		46	47	48
		■						■			

6. **ne midausser netascu** *exp.* in short.

49	50		51	52	53	54	55	56	57	58	59
		■									
60	61	62	63	64	65	66					

7. **lovver cool** *exp.* to drive crazy.

67	68	69	70	71	72		73	74	75	76
						■				

8. **ri de coneisacav** exp. to go on vacation.

77	78		79	80		81	82	83	84	85	86	87	88	89	90

9. **rasehec rásat** *exp.* to back out.

91	92	93	94	95	96	97		98	99	100	101	102

10. **recah sal cesap** *exp.* to make up after a quarrel.

103	104	105	106	107		108	109	110		111	112	113	114	115

Step 2 • Fill in each box below with the letter that corresponds to the number in Step 1 to reveal an expression already learned which means, "by the way."

22	36	37	45	49					
111	112	107	31	63	99	91	96	77	115

ANSWERS TO LESSONS 6-10

LESSON SIX - *Los nuevos vecinos*

Practice the Vocabulary

A. 1. rata
2. faldas
3. luz
4. escupida
5. no sé qué
6. hielo
7. asunto
8. dedo
9. pólvora
10. descosidos
11. papel
12. flote

B. 1. hielo
2. ratón
3. coma
4. descosidos
5. estribos
6. pantalones
7. mano
8. espumarajos, dedo
9. al día
10. estilo

C. 1. D
2. G
3. H
4. I
5. B
6. L
7. J
8. F
9. A
10. K
11. E
12. C

LESSON SEVEN - *El huésped*

Practice the Vocabulary

A. 1. C
   2. H
   3. F
   4. K
   5. J
   6. I
   7. G
   8. L
   9. E
   10. B
   11. A
   12. D

B. 1. b
   2. a
   3. a
   4. c
   5. c
   6. b
   7. c
   8. b
   9. a
   10. a

C. 1. b
   2. b
   3. b
   4. a
   5. b
   6. a
   7. b
   8. b
   9. a
   10. a
   11. a
   12. b

LESSON EIGHT - *El picnic*

Practice the Vocabulary

A. 1. fresco
   2. de remate
   3. molidos
   4. fondo
   5. ratos
   6. clavarle los ojos
   7. cántaros
   8. gatos
   9. pasos
   10. tripas
   11. muriendo
   12. de punta
   13. mira
   14. en cueros
   15. furor

B. 1. lana
    2. verdes, las tripas
    3. todas
    4. pelos
    5. rabo
    6. una vuelta
    7. cuatro
    8. molidos
    9. padre
    10. fondo
    11. las tripas
    12. mira

C. 1. pelos
    2. sopa
    3. verde
    4. cántaros
    5. rabo
    6. vuelta
    7. molidos
    8. tripas
    9. carne
    10. cuatro gatos
    11. boca abajo
    12. pasos
    13. cueros
    14. furor

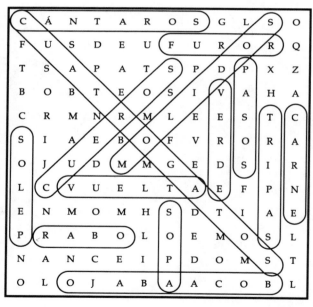

D. 1. C
    2. I
    3. G
    4. E
    5. B
    6. L
    7. K
    8. F
    9. J
    10. H
    11. D
    12. A

LESSON NINE - *Por teléfono*

Practice the Vocabulary

A.
1. C
2. E
3. B
4. J
5. K
6. I
7. F
8. G
9. L
10. A
11. H
12. D
13. N
14. M

B.
1. grano
2. pío
3. vez
4. palo
5. número
6. más
7. rompió
8. borde
9. santo
10. temprano
11. pero
12. carne
13. larga
14. plano

C.
1. D
2. M
3. I
4. N
5. G
6. E
7. A
8. C
9. H
10. L
11. F
12. B
13. K
14. J

D. **Answers to WORD GAME**

1. like father, like son

D	E	■	T	A	L	■	*P*	*A*	*L*	*O*	■	T	A	L
A	S	T	I	L	L	A

2. to interrupt someone

C	O	R	T	A	R	L	E	■	E	L	■	*H*	*I*	*L*	*O*
A	■	A	L	G	U	I	E	N

3. to beat around the bush

A	N	D	A	R	S	E	■	P	O	R	■	L	A	S

R	*A*	*M*	*A*	*S*

4. in the long run

A		L	A	■	C	O	R	T	A	■	O

A		L	A	■	*L*	*A*	*R*	*G*	*A*

5. **1.** to stand someone up • **2.** to leave someone in the lurch

D	E	J	A	R	■	A	L	G	U	I	E	N

P	*L*	*A*	*N*	*T*	*A*	*D*	*O*

6. once and for all

D	E	■	U	N	A	■	V	E	Z	■	Y

P	*A*	*R*	*A*	■	*S*	*I*	*E*	*M*	*P*	*R*	*E*

7. to make a full confession, to spill the beans

C	*A*	*N*	*T*	*A*	*R*	■	*D*	*E*	■	*P*	*L*	*A*	*N*	*O*

8. to begin to, to burst out

R	*O*	*M*	*P*	*E*	*R*	■	*A*

9. behind someone's back

A	■	*E*	*S*	*P*	*A*	*L*	*D*	*A*	*S*	■	D	E

A	L	G	U	I	E	N

10. certainly, of course

D	E	S	D	E	■	*L*	*U*	*E*	*G*	*O*

11. countless

S	*I*	*N*	■	N	Ú	M	E	R	O

"To talk nonstop"

H	A	B	L	A	R	■	*P*	*O*	*R*
L	*O*	*S*	■	*C*	*O*	*D*	*O*	*S*	

LESSON TEN - *De viaje*

Practice the Vocabulary

A.
1. corriente
2. puente
3. rabo
4. paces
5. cuentas, ver
6. gente
7. medias
8. hábito
9. muerto
10. punto, equipaje

B.
1. a
2. b
3. a
4. b
5. b
6. a
7. b
8. a
9. b
10. a
11. b
12. a
13. b
14. a

C. 1. G   7. H

    2. I   8. C

    3. F   9. L

    4. D   10. A

    5. K   11. B

    6. J   12. E

D. **Answers to WORD GAME.**

1. **ed boca a bora** *exp.* from beginning to end.

| 0 D | 1 E | | 2 C | 3 A | 4 B | 5 O | | 6 A | | 7 R | 8 A | 9 B | 10 O |

2. **pro lo sivot** *exp.* by the looks of it.

| 11 P | 12 O | 13 R | | 14 L | 15 O | | 16 V | 17 I | 18 S | 19 T | 20 O |

3. **¿ed sarev?** *exp.* really?

| 21 D | 22 E | | 23 V | 24 E | 25 R | 26 A | 27 S |

4. **herac neupte** *exp.* to take a long weekend.

| 28 H | 29 A | 30 C | 31 E | 32 R | | 33 P | 34 U | 35 E | 36 N | 37 T | 38 E |

5. **on derpo smá** *exp.* to be exhausted.

| 39 N | 40 O | | 41 P | 42 O | 43 D | 44 E | 45 R | | 46 M | 47 Á | 48 S |

6. **ne midausser netascu** *exp.* in short.

| 49 E | 50 N | | 51 R | 52 E | 53 S | 54 U | 55 M | 56 I | 57 D | 58 A | 59 S |
| 60 C | 61 U | 62 E | 63 N | 64 T | 65 A | 66 S | | | | | |

7. **lovver cool** *exp.* to drive crazy.

| 67 V | 68 O | 69 L | 70 V | 71 E | 72 R | ■ | 73 L | 74 O | 75 C | 76 O |

8. **ri de coneisacav** *exp.* to go on vacation.

| 77 I | 78 R | ■ | 79 D | 80 E | ■ | 81 V | 82 A | 83 C | 84 A | 85 C | 86 I | 87 O | 88 N | 89 E | 90 S |

9. **rasehec rásat** *exp.* to back out.

| 91 E | 92 C | 93 H | 94 A | 95 R | 96 S | 97 E | ■ | 98 A | 99 T | 100 R | 101 Á | 102 S |

10. **recah sal cesap** *exp.* to make up after a quarrel.

| 103 H | 104 A | 105 C | 106 E | 107 R | ■ | 108 L | 109 A | 110 S | ■ | 111 P | 112 A | 113 C | 114 E | 115 S |

"By the way"

| 22 E | 36 N | 37 T | 45 R | 49 E |
| 111 P | 112 A | 107 R | 31 É | 63 N | 99 T | 91 E | 96 S | 77 I | 115 S |

REVIEW EXAM
FOR LESSONS 6-10

[Answers to Review Exam, p. 133]

A. Underline the correct translation of the expression in bold.

1. **vivir al día**:
   a. to tolerate
   b. to live from hand to mouth

2. **perder los estribos**:
   a. to lose patience
   b. to lose control

3. **sin faltar una coma**:
   a. down to the last detail
   b. terribly sick

4. **un no sé qué**:
   a. stupid
   b. a certain something

5. **ser otro cantar**:
   a. to sing badly
   b. to be another story

6. **pez gordo**:
   a. to be a fish out of water
   b. bigwig

7. **hacer mal papel**:
   a. to write poorly
   b. to make a bad impression

8. **ratón de biblioteca**:
   a. bookworm
   b. dirty rat

9. **romper el hielo**:
   a. to break the ice
   b. to freeze to death

10. **partirle el corazón a uno**:
    a. to break someone's heart
    b. to break up

11. **a todas luces**:
   a. in good light   b. any way you look at it

12. **dar a luz a**:
   a. to give a light to   b. to give birth to

13. **en fin**:
   a. a fish   b. in short

14. **ir al asunto**:
   a. to get down to the facts   b. to go to work

B. Complete the phrases by choosing the appropriate words from the list below.

adentros	acto	blando
ladilla	añicos	alto
sin más ni más	plantada	Pedro
crisma	lío	abiertos

1. And a como _____ por su casa.

2. Se me pega como una _____ .

3. La dejó _____ .

4. Al principio lo recibí con los brazos _____ .

5. Estaba pensando para mis _____ que le podría pedir
   que se fuera en el _____ pero soy demasiado _____
   de corazón.

6. No solamente eso pero ayer hizo _____ mi florero favorito.

7. ¡Una noche simplemente la dejó _____ !

8. Tengo ganas de romperle la _____ .

9. En buen _____ te has metido.

10. Estaba dispuesto a pasar por _____ algunas de las cosas
    que ha hecho.

C. ANAGRAM - Solve the message in three steps.

Step 1 • Find the eight expressions that all mean "in a jiffy" from the list below by crossing out the two that don't belong in the group. [See Chapter 8 - Vocabulary listing under *a toda prisa* p. 89]

en un avemaría

en un chiflido

en un credo

en un decir Jesús

en un dos por tres

en un improviso

en un salto

en un puño

en un burro

en un soplo

Step 2 • The correct expressions are scrambled below. Write the unscrambled words in the boxes on the right. The first one has been done for you. By the way, the words "en un" have not been included in the following expressions.

1. DFILOHCI

1 C	2 H	3 I	4 F	5 L	6 I	7 D	8 O

2. PLOOS

9	10	11	12	13

3. TALSO

14	15	16	17	18

4. RAMEAVÍA

19	20	21	22	23	24	25	26

5. DOREC

27	28	29	30	31

6. CRIDEJSESÚ

32	33	34	35	36	37	38	39	40	41

7. PRERODSTOS

42	43	44	45	46	47	48	49	50	51

8. SIPORVIMO

52	53	54	55	56	57	58	59	60

Step 3 • **Find the missing expression which also means "in a jiffy." Simply fill in each box below with the letter that corresponds to the number in Step 2. Some of the letters have already been given to you.**

21 N		22	29 N	10	9		Q	U	29	
27	15 N	17	26		U	N	G	23	5	5	60

D. Match the English with the Spanish.

☐ 1. I'm starving.

☐ 2. Restaurants always rip you off.

☐ 3. Dirty old men make my stomach turn.

☐ 4. Be on the lookout.

☐ 5. I love doing that in my spare time.

☐ 6. I'm dying to go on a picnic.

☐ 7. I feel like taking a stroll through the park.

☐ 8. It would be nice to get some fresh air.

☐ 9. There's hardly anyone here.

☐ 10. The guy must have been nuts.

☐ 11. My hair stood on end.

☐ 12. It's been raining buckets for an hour.

☐ 13. I was soaking wet.

☐ 14. I was exhausted.

A. **Se me pusieron los cabellos de punta.**

B. **Ha estado lloviendo a cántaros por una hora.**

C. **Me crujen las tripas.**

D. **Tenía los huesos molidos.**

E. **Tengo ganas de dar una vuelta por el parque.**

F. **Los viejos verdes me revuelven las tripas.**

G. **Estaba hecho una sopa.**

H. **Los restaurantes siempre te clavan la lana.**

I. **No hay ni cuatro gatos aquí.**

J. **El tipo tenía que estar loco de remate.**

K. **Hay que estar a la mira.**

L. **Sería padre tomar un poco de aire fresco.**

M. **Me gusta hacer eso en mis ratos libres.**

N. **Me estoy muriendo de ganas por ir de picnic.**

E. Underline the appropriate word(s) that best complete(s) the phrase.

1. Siempre te andas por las (**ramas, rameras**).

2. No hay (**perro, pero**) que valga.

3. ¡Qué fantasmas ni qué (**dos, ocho**) cuartos!

4. No te quiero cortar el (**grito, hielo, hilo**) pero si me pasara a mí, me darían deseos de saltarme la (**tapa, rama, uña**) de los sesos.

5. Seguro que estaba al (**bueno, borde**) del llanto.

6. Ya ve al (**grito, grano**).

7. No te quiero cortar el (**hilo, hielo**) pero si me pasara a mí, me darían deseos de saltarme la (**talla, tapa**) de los sesos.

8. A que ya estaba saliendo con otra a (**pies, espaldas**) de ella.

9. Tú sabes que él siempre ha tenido novias sin (**palabras, número**).

10. Una noche la dejó (**planchada, plantada**).

11. De tal palo, tal (**pastilla, astilla**).

12. Su padre y él son (**uña, una**) y carne.

13. Cantará de (**plano, piano**).

14. Tarde o (**temporal, temprano**) iba a pasar.

ANSWERS TO REVIEW EXAM FOR LESSONS 6-10

A. 1. b
    2. b
    3. a
    4. b
    5. b
    6. b
    7. b
    8. a
    9. a
    10. a
    11. b
    12. b
    13. b
    14. a

B. 1. Pedro
    2. ladilla
    3. sin más ni más
    4. abiertos
    5. adentros, acto, blando
    6. añicos
    7. plantada
    8. crisma
    9. lío
    10. alto

C. **Answer to WORD GAME**

1. DFILOHCI

¹C	²H	³I	⁴F	⁵L	⁶I	⁷D	⁸O

2. PLOOS

⁹S	¹⁰O	¹¹P	¹²L	¹³O

3. TALSO

¹⁴S	¹⁵A	¹⁶L	¹⁷T	¹⁸O

4. RAMEAVÍA

¹⁹A	²⁰V	²¹E	²²M	²³A	²⁴R	²⁵Í	²⁶A

5. DOREC

²⁷C	²⁸R	²⁹E	³⁰D	³¹O

6. CRIDEJSESÚ

³²D	³³E	³⁴C	³⁵I	³⁶R	³⁷J	³⁸E	³⁹S	⁴⁰Ú	⁴¹S

7. PRERODSTOS

⁴²D	⁴³O	⁴⁴S	⁴⁵P	⁴⁶O	⁴⁷R	⁴⁸T	⁴⁹R	⁵⁰E	⁵¹S

8. SIPORVIMO

⁵²I	⁵³M	⁵⁴P	⁵⁵R	⁵⁶O	⁵⁷V	⁵⁸I	⁵⁹S	⁶⁰O

"In a jiffy"

²¹E	N		²²M	²⁹E	N	¹⁰O	⁹S		Q	U	²⁹E	
²⁷C	¹⁵A	N	¹⁷T	²⁶A		U	N		²³G	⁵A	⁵L	⁶⁰O

D. 1. C
   2. H
   3. F
   4. K
   5. M
   6. N
   7. E
   8. L
   9. I
   10. J
   11. A
   12. B
   13. G
   14. D

E. 1. ramas
   2. pero
   3. ocho
   4. hilo, tapa
   5. borde
   6. grano
   7. hilo, tapa
   8. espaldas
   9. número
   10. plantada
   11. astilla
   12. uña
   13. plano
   14. temprano

LESSON ELEVEN

El partido de fútbol

(The Soccer Game)

Vaya, ¿y tú qué haces aquí?

Voy a verme con Julio aquí pero tengo que admitir que me siento como pez fuera del agua.

EL PARTIDO DE FÚTBOL...

DIÁLOGO

Simón se encuentra con Donato en el partido de fútbol.

Donato:	**Vaya**, ¿y tú qué haces aquí?
Simón:	Voy a **verme con** Julio aquí pero tengo que admitir que me siento **como (un) pez fuera del agua**. No sé nada sobre este deporte.
Donato:	No puedo creer que verdaderamente viniste **a las buenas**, pero **ver es creer**.
Simón:	**A decir verdad**, vengo solamente **de cuando en cuando**. Sabes, llegué **en menos que canta un gallo** pero después me tomó media hora **abrirme paso** entre la muchedumbre. Me sorprende habérmelas arreglado para llegar **a la hora**. ¿Qué hora es?
Donato:	Ahora **son como** las 2:00. Siempre empiezan a jugar a las 2:00 **en punto**. Sabes, estas localidades son buenísimas. La vez anterior **no pude ver gota**.
Simón:	¿Conoces a ese jugador **narizón**? El que se **da lija**. Tengo su nombre **en la punta de la lengua**… ¿Juan Vásquez?
Donato:	Su nombre **no me suena**. Ah sí, el que juega **malísimamente**.
Simón:	**¡Qué va!**
Donato:	¡Pero sí **salta a la vista**! No seas **testarudo**. Te estás **haciendo ilusiones** si crees que él sabe jugar bien. Debieran **darle de baja** del equipo. **No ve un burro a tres pasos**.
Simón:	Bueno, pero **en cambio** se esfuerza mucho. No creo que haya **nacido parado**. **De hecho**, la última vez que lo vi **se cayó de narices**. ¡A que **vio las estrellas**!

THE SOCCER GAME...

DIALOGUE

Simón runs into Donato at the soccer game.

Donato: Hey, what are you doing here?

Simón: I'm going to meet Julio here but I've got to admit that I feel like a fish out of water. I don't know a thing about this game.

Donato: I can't believe you actually came here willingly, but seeing is believing!

Simón: To tell you the truth, I only come here occasionally. You know, I got here in no time at all although it took me a half hour to make my way through the crowd. I'm surprised I was able to make it in time. What time is it?

Donato: It's about 2:00. They always start these games at 2:00 sharp. You know, these are great seats. Last time I couldn't see a thing.

Simón: You know that player with the huge nose? The one with the attitude. I have his name on the tip of my tongue... Juan Vásquez?

Donato: His name doesn't ring a bell. Oh, yeah, the one who's a lousy player.

Simón: Get out of here!

Donato: But it's obvious! Don't be so stubborn. You're kidding yourself if you think he knows how to play well. They should just drop him from the team. He's as blind as a bat.

Simón: Okay, but on the other hand, he does try hard. I don't think he was born lucky. In fact, last time I saw him, he fell right on his face. I bet he saw stars!

Literal Translation of Dialogue

DIALOGUE

Simón runs into Donato at the soccer game.

Donato: Go on, and you what are you doing here?

Simón: I came to see me with Julio here but I have to admit that I feel like a fish out of water. I don't know anything about this sport.

Donato: I can't believe that you actually came to the good ones, but to see is to believe.

Simón: To say truth, I come only from when to when. You know, I arrived in less (time) than a rooster sings but later it took me half an hour to open passage through the crowd. I'm surprised I managed to arrive at the hour. What time is it?

Donato: Now they are like 2:00. They always start to play at 2:00 on the dot. You know, these seats are really great. The last time I couldn't see a drop.

Simón: Do you know that player with the huge nose? The one who gives himself sandpaper. I have his name on the point of the tongue... Juan Vásquez?

Donato: His name doesn't sound to me. Oh, yeah, the one who plays so badly.

Simón: What goes!

Donato: But it jumps to the sight! Don't be heady. You're making yourself illusions if you believe he knows how to play well. They should just give him from under the team. He doesn't see a donkey from three steps.

Simón: Good, but in exchange he tries hard. I don't think he was born standing. Of fact, the last time I saw him he fell on his nose. I bet he saw stars!

VOCABULARY

a decir verdad *exp.* to tell (you) the truth • (lit); to say the truth.

a la hora *exp.* on time, punctually • (lit); on the hour • *Llegó a la hora;* He/She arrived on time.
ALSO: **a buena hora** *exp.* at an opportune time • (lit); at good hour.

a las buenas/malas *exp.* willingly/unwillingly • (lit); in a good/bad way.
SYNONYM (1): **por las buenas/malas** *exp.* • (lit); for the good/bad ones.
SYNONYM (2): **por las buenas o por las malas** *exp.* whether one likes it or not • (lit); for the good or for the bad ones.
SYNONYM (3): **de mangas o de faldas** *exp.* (Ecuador) • (lit); from sleeves or from skirts.

abrirse paso *exp.* to work one's way through (a crowd, etc.) • (lit); to open passage.

caer de narices *exp.* to fall on one's face • (lit); to fall on one's nose.

como (un) pez fuera del agua *exp.* to feel out of place, to feel like a fish out of water • (lit); like a fish out of water.
SYNONYM (1): **estar como perro en barrio ajeno** *exp.* • (lit); to be like a dog in a strange neighborhood.
SYNONYM (2): **estar como gallina en corral ajeno** *exp.* • (lit); to be like a chicken in a strange pen.

dar de baja *exp.* to drop (from a team, list, etc.), dismiss, discharge, fire • (lit); to give from under.
ALSO: **por lo bajo** *exp.* on the sly.

darse lija *exp.* (Cuba, Puerto Rico, Dominican Republic) to put on airs, to act pretentious • (lit); to give oneself sandpaper.
SYNONYM (1): **darse tono** *exp.* • (lit); to give oneself tone (or "to give off a pretentious tone").
SYNONYM (2): **subirse de tono** *exp.* • (lit); to get on a tone.
SYNONYM (3): **darse mucho taco** *exp.* (Mexico) • (lit); to give oneself much heel.
SYNONYM (4): **botarse el pucho** *exp.* (Chile) • (lit); to bounce a cigarette.
SYNONYM (5): **darse corte/darse paquete** *exp.* (Ecuador) • (lit); to give oneself length/to give oneself package.

de cuando en cuando *exp.* sometimes, occasionally • (lit); from when to when.
SYNONYM: **de vez en cuando** *exp.* • (lit); from time to when.

de hecho *exp.* in fact • (lit); of fact.

en cambio *exp.* but, on the other hand • (lit); in exchange.

en menos que canta un gallo *exp.* in a flash, in a jiffy, in two shakes of a lamb's tail • (lit); in less (time) than a rooster sings (crows).
ALSO: **entre gallos y media noche** *exp.* at an unearthly hour • (lit); between roosters and midnight.

en punto *exp.* on the dot, sharp • (lit); on the point.

hacerse ilusiones *exp.* to fool oneself, to delude oneself • (lit); to make oneself illusions.

malísimamente *adv.* very badly, terribly.
NOTE: This comes from the adverb *mal* meaning "poorly."

nacer parado(a) *exp.* to be born lucky • (lit); to be born standing.

narizón *adj.* big-nosed.
NOTE (1): This comes from the feminine noun *nariz* meaning "nose." In Spanish, special suffixes are commonly attached to nouns, adjectives, and adverbs to intensify their meaning. In this case, the suffix *zón* is added to the word *nariz*, transforming it into *narizón* or "honker, schnozzola, etc." In saying "Look at his big nose!" it would certainly be more colloquial to say *¡Mira su narizón!* rather than *¡Mira su gran nariz!* The same would apply to other nouns as well, such as *cabeza* meaning "head": *¡Mira su cabezón!* rather than *¡Mira su gran cabeza!*
NOTE (2): When a noun is modified using the suffix *zón*, it may be used interchangeably as an adjective:

NOUN ⟹	MODIFIED NOUN ⟹	MODIFIED ADJECTIVE
¡Mira su nariz!	*¡Mira su narizón!*	*Es un tipo narizón.*
(Look at his nose!)	(Look at his big honker!)	(He's a big-nosed guy.)
¡Mira su cabeza!	*¡Mira su cabezón!*	*Es un tipo cabezón.*
(Look at his head!)	(Look at his big head!)	(He's a big-headed guy.)

no poder ver gota *exp.* not to be able to see a thing • (lit); not to be able to see a drop.

no ver un burro a tres pasos *exp.* to be as blind as a bat • (lit); not to see a donkey at three paces.
ALSO: burro *m.* dumb • (lit); donkey.

¡Qué va! *exclam.* Baloney! No way! Get out of here! • (lit); What goes!
SYNONYM (1): **¡Qué disparate!** *exclam.* What baloney!
SYNONYM (2): **¡Qué tontería!** *exclam.* What stupidity!
SYNONYM (3): **¡Qué bobada!** *exclam.* What nonsense!

saltar a la vista *exp.* to be obvious • (lit); to jump to the sight.
SYNONYM: **saltar a los ojos** *exp.* • (lit); to jump to the eyes.

son como *exp.* used when indicating an approximate time, i.e. *Son como las 5:00*; It's around 5:00 • SEE: **en punto**

sonarle *v.* to sound familiar (to one), to ring a bell (in one's memory) • (lit); to sound to one.
ALSO: **sonarse** *v.* to blow one's nose • (lit); to sound oneself • NOTE: This is short for *sonarse las narices* which literally means "to sound the nostrils."

tener en la punta de la lengua *exp.* • (lit); to have on the tip of the tongue.

testarudo(a) *adj.* stubborn, headstrong.
NOTE: This comes from the feminine noun *testa* meaning "head."
SYNONYM: **cabezón** *adj.* **1.** headstrong • **2.** big-headed • NOTE: This comes from the feminine noun *cabeza* meaning "head."

¡Vaya! *interj.* **1.** (used to indicate surprise) Well! How about that! • **2.** (commonly used to modify a noun) *¡Vaya equipo!*; What a team! / *¡Vaya calor!*; What heat! • **3.** (used to impact a statement) *Es buen tipo, ¡vaya!*; He's a really good guy! • (lit); Go!
SYNONYM: **¡Vamos!** *interj.* • (lit); Go! *Vamos* can also be used within a sentence to indicate that the speaker has just changed his/her mind or is making a clarification. In this case, *vamos* is translated as "well": *Es guapa... vamos, no es fea*; She's pretty... well, she's not ugly.
NOTE: Both *vaya* and *vamos* are extremely popular and both come from the verb *ir* meaning "to go."

ver es creer *exp.* seeing is believing • (lit); to see is to believe.
SYNONYM: **ver para creer** *exp.* • (lit); to see in order to believe.

ver las estrellas *exp.* • (lit); to see the stars.
ALSO (1): **nacer con buena estrella** *exp.* to be born under a lucky star • (lit); to be born with good star.
ALSO (2): **nacer con estrella** *exp.* to be born under a lucky star • (lit); to be born with star.

verse con *exp.* to meet • (lit); to see oneself with.

PRACTICE THE VOCABULARY

[Answers to Lesson 11, p. 188]

A. Underline the correct definition of the expression given.

1. **de cuando en cuando:**
   a. sometimes   b. never

2. **a la hora:**
   a. late   b. on time

3. **nacer parado:**
   a. to be born unlucky   b. to be born lucky

4. **a las buenas:**
   a. a good time   b. willingly

5. **caer de narices:**
   a. to break one's nose   b. to fall on one's face

6. **no ver gota:**
   a. not to see a thing   b. to fall on one's face

7. **testarudo:**
   a. testy   b. stubborn

8. **verse con:**
   a. to dislike someone   b. to meet someone

9. **sonarle:**
   a. to ring one's chimes   b. to sound familiar

10. **saltar a la vista:**
    a. to be obvious   b. to sound familiar

11. **darse lija:**
    a. to put on airs   b. to fire from office

12. **en punto:**
    a. late   b. on the dot

B. Complete the sentences by choosing the appropriate words from the list below.

suena	**verme**	**buenas**
en cuando	**canta un gallo**	**paso**
punto	**gota**	**lija**
punta	**vista**	**ilusiones**

1. Te estás haciendo _____ si crees que él sabe jugar bien.

2. Voy a _____ con Julio aquí.

3. Siempre empiezan a jugar a las 2:00 en _____ .

4. No puedo creer que verdaderamente viniste a las _____ .

5. Sabes, llegué en menos que _____ .

6. Vengo solamente de cuando _____ .

7. Me tomó media hora abrirme _____ entre la muchedumbre.

8. ¡Salta a la _____ !

9. La vez anterior no pude ver ni _____ .

10. ¿Conoces a ese jugador? El que se da _____ .

11. Tengo el nombre en la _____ de la lengua.

12. Su nombre no me _____ .

C. Match the columns.

☐ 1. Hey, what are you doing here?

☐ 2. Get out of here!

☐ 3. I bet he saw stars!

☐ 4. In fact, last time I saw him, he fell right on his face.

☐ 5. Don't be so stubborn.

☐ 6. I feel like a fish out of water.

☐ 7. To tell you the truth, I only come here occasionally.

☐ 8. I'm surprised I was able to make it on time.

☐ 9. He's as blind as a bat.

☐ 10. Last time I couldn't see a thing.

☐ 11. You're fooling yourself.

☐ 12. On the other hand, he does try hard.

A. **No ve un burro a tres pasos.**

B. **Te estás haciendo ilusiones.**

C. **Me siento como (un) pez fuera del agua.**

D. **De hecho, la última vez que lo vi se cayó de narices.**

E. **Vaya, ¿y tú qué haces aquí?**

F. **La vez anterior no pude ver gota.**

G. **En cambio se esfuerza mucho.**

H. **¡Qué va!**

I. **No seas tan testarudo.**

J. **A decir verdad, vengo aquí solamente de cuando en cuando.**

K. **¡A que vio las estrellas!**

L. **Me sorprende habérmelas arreglado para llegar a la hora.**

D. Fill in the crossword puzzle on page 147 by using the words from the list below.

verdad	vista	narices
paso	punto	parado
ilusiones	narizón	sonar
ver		

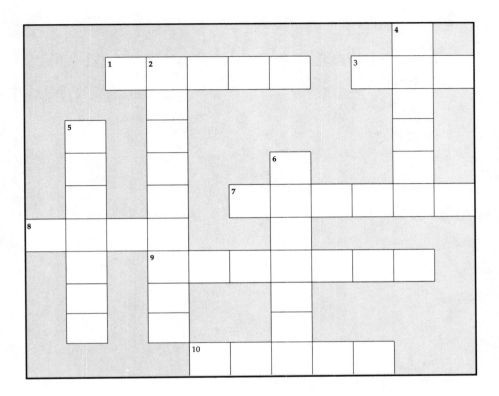

ACROSS

1. **saltar a la** _____ *exp.* to be obvious

3. _____ **es creer** *exp.* seeing is believing

7. **nacer** _____ *exp.* to be born lucky

8. **abrirse** _____ *exp.* to work one's way through (a crowd, etc.)

9. **caer de** _____ *exp.* to fall on one's face

10. **en** _____ *exp.* on the dot

DOWN

2. **hacerse** _____ *exp.* to fool oneself

4. **a decir** _____ *exp.* to tell (you) the truth

5. _____ *v.* to sound familiar

6. _____ *m. & adj.* **1.** big nose • **2.** big-nosed

LESSON TWELVE

El cine

(The Movies)

Me estoy muriendo de aburrimiento.
Vamos a ver una película de horror.

EL CINE...

DIÁLOGO

Cecilia y Nancy están tratando de decidir lo que van a hacer un sábado por la noche.

Cecilia:	Me estoy **muriendo de aburrimiento**. Vamos a ver una película de horror.
Nancy:	Detesto las películas de horror.
Cecilia:	Bueno, **cada loco con su tema**. En ese caso, vamos a ver la nueva película al cine.
Nancy:	¿De qué **se trata** la película?
Cecilia:	No sé.
Nancy:	¿Y entonces cómo te **enteraste**?
Cecilia:	Nada más **he oído decir que** es buenísima. **Se está haciendo noche** así que vamos a tener que irnos enseguida.
Nancy:	**Me revienta** tener que gastar tanto dinero. Yo **no estoy podrida en dinero** como tú. Vamos a hacer algo diferente.
Cecilia:	No te preocupes, **chica**, que yo voy a pagar.
Nancy:	La verdad es que siempre **estás con la misma cantaleta**. Además, no tenemos carro.
Cecilia:	Usaremos el de mi madre. Voy a tratar de **darle coba**.
Nancy:	Hazle un **cuento chino**; no sé, que me tienes que llevar al médico o algo **por el estilo**.
Cecilia:	O simplemente podemos ir en su carro sin decirle nada. Creo que está **echando un sueño**. Además, es **dura de oído**.
Nancy:	¡Tú estás **más loca que una chiva**! Tú sabes que ella **tiene mal genio**. Y nos podría **salir el tiro por la culata**. Te gusta **meterte entre las patas de los caballos**, ¿verdad? Tú sabes lo que diría tu madre, **"Cría cuervos y te sacarán los ojos."** Me **da lo mismo** si vamos más tarde. En vez de **ir al cine**, vamos a jugar a las cartas.
Cecilia:	Pero es una película **chévere** y **vale la pena** verla. **De un modo u otro**, tenemos que ir.

THE MOVIES...

DIALOGUE

Cecilia and Nancy are trying to figure out what to do on a Saturday night.

Cecilia:	I'm bored to death. Let's go see a horror movie.
Nancy:	I hate horror movies.
Cecilia:	Well, to each his own. In that case, let's go see the new film at the movie theater.
Nancy:	What's the film about?
Cecilia:	I don't know.
Nancy:	Well, how did you find out about it?
Cecilia:	I just heard that it's great. It's getting late so we're going to have to go right away.
Nancy:	It bothers me to have to spend so much money. I'm not filthy rich like you. Let's do something else.
Cecilia:	Don't worry, pal, I'll pay.
Nancy:	You really do have a one-track mind. Besides, we don't have a car.
Cecilia:	Let's use my mother's. I'll try to butter her up.
Nancy:	Just tell her some cock-and-bull story; I don't know, that you have to take me to the doctor or something like that.
Cecilia:	Or we could just go in her car without telling her anything. I think she's taking a nap. Besides, she's hard of hearing.
Nancy:	You're out of your mind! You know she's got a bad temper. And the whole thing could backfire. You really like getting into trouble, huh? You know what your mother would say, "Don't bite the hand that feeds you." It's all the same to me if we go later. Instead of going to the movies, let's go play cards.
Cecilia:	But it's a neat movie and worth seeing. Somehow, we have to go.

Literal Translation of Dialogue

DIALOGUE

Cecilia and Nancy are trying to figure out what to do on a Saturday night.

Cecilia: I'm dying of boredom. Let's go see a horror movie.

Nancy: I hate horror movies.

Cecilia: Well, each lunatic with his theme. In that case, let's go the new film at the movie theater.

Nancy: What does the movie deal with?

Cecilia: I don't know.

Nancy: Well, how did you inform yourself?

Cecilia: I just heard it said that it's great. It's getting late so we're going to have to go immediately.

Nancy: I burst to have to spend so much money. I'm not rotten in money like you. Let's do something different.

Cecilia: Don't worry, girl, because I'm going to pay.

Nancy: The truth is you're always with the same serenade. Besides, we don't have a car.

Cecilia: Let's use my mother's. I'm going to try giving her flattery.

Nancy: Tell her a Chinese story; I don't know, that you have to take me to the doctor or something for the style.

Cecilia: Or we could just go in her car without saying anything to her. I think she's throwing a nap. Besides, she's hard of hearing.

Nancy: You're as crazy as a young goat! You know she's got a bad disposition. And it could get shot out of the breech (or butt of a firearm). You really like putting yourself between the feet of the horses, true? You know what your mother would say, "Feed crows and they take your eyes out." It gives me the same if we go later. In time of going to the movies, let's go play cards.

Cecilia: But it's a neat movie and worth the pain to see it. Of one mode or another, we have to go.

VOCABULARY

cada loco con su tema *exp.* to each his own • (lit); each lunatic with his/her theme.
SYNONYM (1): **para gustos se han hecho colores** *exp.* • (lit); for tastes colors have been made.
SYNONYM (2): **cada perico a su estaca, cada chango a su mecate** *exp.* • (lit); each parakeet (or parrot) to his perch, each monkey to his cord.

cría cuervos y te sacarán los ojos *exp.* that's the thanks you get, to bite the hand that feeds you • (lit); raise crows and they will take out your eyes.

cuento chino *exp.* cock-and-bull story • (lit); a Chinese story.

chévere *adj.* (Cuba, Puerto Rico, Dominican Republic) terrific, neat.

chico(a) *n.* (Cuba, Puerto Rico, Dominican Republic) pal, chum, kid • (lit); boy/girl • *¡Hola, chico!* Hi, kid!
SYNONYM: **hermano(a)** *n.* • (lit); brother/sister • *¡Mi hermano!* Hey pal!

dar lo mismo *exp.* to make no difference • (lit); to give the same.

darle coba a uno *exp.* to soft-soap someone, to suck up to someone • (lit); to give flattery to someone.

¿de qué se trata? *exp.* what's it about? what does it deal with? • (lit); of what does it discuss/deal?

de un modo u otro *exp.* one way or another, somehow • (lit); of one manner or another.

echar un sueño *exp.* to take a nap • (lit); to throw a sleep.
SYNONYM (1): **tomar una siestesita** *exp.* to take a little nap • (lit); to throw/sleep a little siesta.
SYNONYM (2): **echar/dormir una siestesita** *exp.* (Cuba, Puerto Rico, Dominican Republic) • (lit); to throw/sleep a little nap.
SYNONYM (3): **tomar una pestañita** *exp.* (Mexico) to get some shut-eye • (lit); to take a little eyelash.
SYNONYM (4): **dormir la siesta** *exp.* • (lit); to sleep the nap.
SYNONYM (5): **echar un pestañazo** *exp.* (Cuba, Puerto Rico, Dominican Republic).
ALSO (1): **dormir a pierna suelta** *exp.* to sleep soundly • (lit); to sleep with loose legs.
ALSO (2): **pasar la noche en claro/en blanco** *exp.* not to sleep a wink • (lit); to spend the night in brightness/in blank.
ALSO (3): **dormir como un lirón** *exp.* to sleep like a log • (lit); to sleep like a dormouse.

ALSO (4): **dormir como un tronco** *exp.* to sleep like a log • (lit); to sleep like a trunk (of a tree).

ALSO (5): **estar en los brazos de Morfeo** *exp.* to sleep soundly • (lit); to be in the arms of Morpheus (the son of sleep and the god of dreams, according to Ovid).

enterarse *v.* to find out, to get to know • (lit); to inform oneself.

estar podrido(a) en dinero *exp.* to be filthy-rich, stinking-rich • (lit); to be rotten in money.

SYNONYM (1): **tener más lana que un borrego** *exp.* • (lit); to have more wool than a lamb • NOTE: This is actually a humorous play on words since the feminine noun *lana*, which literally translates as "wool," is also used to connote "money, loot, dough." An equivalent expression might be, "He has more dough than a baker."

SYNONYM (2): **tener el riñón bien cubierto** *exp.* • (lit); to have a well-covered kidney.

SYNONYM (3): **estar bien parado(a)** *exp.* • (lit); to be standing up well.

SYNONYM (4): **tener la canasta baja y el riñón bien cubierto** *exp.* (Mexico) • (lit); to have the basket low and the kidney well-covered.

estar siempre con la misma cantaleta *exp.* to harp on the same string, to have a one-track mind • (lit); to be always with the same serenade.

SYNONYM: **estar siempre con la misma letanía** *exp.* • (lit); to be always with the same litany.

hacerse noche *exp.* to get dark, to get late in the afternoon • (lit); to make itself (to become) night.

SYNONYM: **hacerse tarde** *exp.* to become late • (lit); to make itself late.

ir al cine *exp.* to go to the movies • (lit); to go to the movie house.

más loco(a) que un(a) chivo(a) *exp.* (Cuba, Puerto Rico, Dominican Republic) to be out of one's mind, to be crazy • (lit); to be crazier than a young goat.

meterse entre las patas de los caballos *exp.* to get into trouble • (lit); to put oneself between the horses' feet.

morirse de aburrimiento *exp.* to be bored to death, bored stiff • (lit); to die of boredom.

SYNONYM: **aburrirse como una ostra** *exp.* • (lit); to bore oneself like an oyster.

oír hablar de *exp.* to hear of (something) • (lit); to hear speak of (something).
NOTE: Many students of Spanish make the common mistake of using *oír de* instead of *oír hablar de*. Although the literation translation of *oír de* is indeed "to hear of," this is not a correct Spanish expression. For example: *He oído hablar de ella;* "I've heard of her." It would *not* be correct to say: *He oído de ella.* The same holds true for the expression *oír decir que* not *oír que,* another common mistake made by Spanish students who are trying to say "to hear that." For example: *He oído decir que su mamá está enferma;* I've heard (say) that her/his mother is sick. It would *not* be correct to say: *He oído que su mamá está enferma.*

reventar *v.* **1.** to annoy, to bother, to irritate • **2.** to tire someone out • (lit); to burst.

salir el tiro por la culata *exp.* to backfire • (lit); to have the shot go out the breech or butt (of a firearm).

ser duro(a) de oído *exp.* to be hard of hearing • (lit); to be hard of hearing.
SYNONYM: **ser sordo(a) como una tapia** *exp.* • (lit); to be deaf as a wall.

tener mal genio *exp.* to have a bad temper • (lit); to have a bad disposition.
SYNONYM: **tener un geniazo horrible** *exp.* • (lit); to have a horrible disposition.

valer la pena *exp.* to be worthwhile • (lit); to be worth the pain.

PRACTICE THE VOCABULARY

[Answers to Lesson 12, p. 189]

A. Complete the sentences by choosing the appropriate words from the list below.

tema	revienta	coba
chino	estilo	duro
chivo	genio	culata
caballos	cuervos	mismo

1. Cría _____ y te sacarán los ojos.

2. Voy a tratar de darle _____ .

3. Cada loco con su _____ .

4. Me da lo _____ si vamos más tarde.

5. Hazle un cuento _____ .

6. Podría salir el tiro por la _____ .

7. Me _____ tener que gastar tanto dinero.

8. Es _____ de oído.

9. Te gusta meterte entre las patas de los _____ , ¿verdad?

10. Tú sabes que ella tiene mal _____ .

11. Dile que me tienes que llevar al médico o algo por el _____ .

12. ¡Tú estás más loco que un _____ !

B. Underline the correct definition of the words in boldface.

1. **estar podrido en dinero:**
   a. to be broke
   b. to be filthy-rich

2. **chévere:**
   a. terrific
   b. terrible

3. **reventar:**
   a. to bother, irritate
   b. to love

4. **estar siempre con la misma cantaleta:**
   a. to complain
   b. to harp

5. **dar lo mismo:**
   a. to rake someone over the coals
   b. to make no difference

6. **salir el tiro por la culata:**
   a. to backfire
   b. to work out well

7. **meterse entre las patas de los caballos:**
   a. to go horseback riding
   b. to get into trouble

8. **tener mal genio:**
   a. to have a bad temper
   b. to have a horrible headache

9. **valer la pena:**
   a. to be painful
   b. to be worthwhile

10. **enterarse:**
    a. to forget   b. to find out

11. **cuento chino:**
    a. funny story   b. cock-and-bull story

12. **darle coba a uno:**
    a. to rake someone over the coals   b. to soft-soap someone

C. Match the columns.

☐ 1. You have a one-track mind.

☐ 2. It's all the same to me if we go later.

☐ 3. It's a great movie and worth it.

☐ 4. What's the movie about?

☐ 5. I've heard it's fabulous.

☐ 6. I think she's taking a nap.

☐ 7. Don't worry about it, kiddo.

☐ 8. It's getting dark.

☐ 9. Somehow, we have to go.

☐ 10. I'll try to butter her up.

☐ 11. Let's go to the movies.

☐ 12. I'm bored to death.

A. **Me estoy muriendo de aburrimiento.**

B. **Creo que ella está echando un sueño.**

C. **De un modo u otro, tenemos que ir.**

D. **¿De qué se trata la película?**

E. **He oído decir que es fabulosa.**

F. **Es una película chévere y vale la pena.**

G. **Se está haciendo noche.**

H. **Siempre estás con la misma cantaleta.**

I. **No te preocupes, chica.**

J. **Voy a tratar de darle coba.**

K. **Me da lo mismo si vamos más tarde.**

L. **Vamos al cine.**

LESSON THIRTEEN

En el rastro

(At the Flea Market)

¡Chelita! Y tú, ¿qué haces aquí?

Vine a fin de buscar un regalo para mi novio. Además, es el cumpleaños de mi futura suegra y así mato dos pájaros de un tiro.

EN EL RASTRO...

DIÁLOGO

Déborah se encuentra con Chelita en el rastro.

Déborah:	¡Chelita! Y tú, ¿qué haces aquí?
Chelita:	Vine **a fin de** buscar un regalo para mi novio. Además, es el cumpleaños de mi futura suegra y así **mato dos pájaros de un tiro**.
Déborah:	Yo creía que ustedes **se llevaban como perro y gato**.
Chelita:	No hay duda alguna que yo no **soy la niña de sus ojos** pero pensé que si **la colmo de** regalos quizás empezaremos a **llevarnos bien**. A lo mejor hasta **se le hace un nudo en la garganta**. Lo que no quiero hacer es **echar la casa por la ventana**. En todo caso, **me he estado rompiendo la cabeza** tratando de encontrar los regalos perfectos. No quiero **dejar piedra por mover**. En cuanto a Tom, lo **conozco como la palma de mi mano** pero sencillamente no sé lo que a ella le gusta. Ese suéter allí sí que me gusta mucho.
Déborah:	Pero no está **de moda**. Se ve muy **corriente** y además parece ser **de pacotilla**. Pero **para gustos se han hecho colores**. Por lo menos estoy segura que le va a **quedar bien**.
Chelita:	Lo único que quiero es encontrar algo **de primera**.
Déborah:	Allí está esa vendedora **bizca**. Se pasa la vida **brava**. Siempre **se me ha atravesado**.
Chelita:	Me pregunto si **empina el codo**. Mire ese vestido allí; ¡está bello! Quizás me lo dé a mitad del precio si la trato bien.
Déborah:	**¡Qué boba eres! ¡Estás en las nubes!**
Chelita:	Tienes razón. ¿Sabes qué? Voy a comprar los regalos la semana que viene cuando tenga más ánimo. **Más vale tarde que nunca**.

Lesson Thirteen

AT THE FLEA MARKET...

DIALOGUE

Déborah runs into Chelita at the flea market.

Déborah: Chelita! What are you doing here?

Chelita: I came here in order to find a gift for my fiancé. Plus, it's my future mother-in-law's birthday so I can kill two birds with one stone.

Déborah: I thought you two didn't get along.

Chelita: I'm definitely not the apple of her eye, but I figured that if I shower her with gifts, maybe we'll start to get along. Maybe she'll even get a lump in her throat. I just don't want to go overboard. Anyway, I've been racking my brains trying to find the perfect gifts. I don't want to leave any stone unturned. As for Tom, I know him backwards and forwards but I just don't know what she likes. I really like that sweater over there.

Déborah: But it's just not stylish. It's really run-of-the-mill and looks cheap besides. But to each his own. At least, I'm sure it would fit well.

Chelita: All I want is to find something first-rate.

Déborah: There's that cross-eyed saleswoman. She's always in a bad mood. I've always had a grudge against her.

Chelita: I wonder if she takes a nip or two on the job. Look at that dress over there; it's beautiful! If I'm nice to her maybe she'll give it to me at half price.

Déborah: How silly you are! You're daydreaming.

Chelita: You're right. You know what? I'll just buy the presents next week when I have more energy. Better late than never.

Literal Translation of Dialogue

DIALOGUE

Déborah finds herself with Chelita at the flea market.

Déborah:	Chelita! And what are you doing here?
Chelita:	I came to the end of finding a gift for my fiancé. Besides, it's my future mother-in-law's birthday so I can kill two birds with one throw.
Déborah:	I thought you two carried yourselves like dog and cat.
Chelita:	There is no doubt that I'm not the apple of her eye, but I thought that if I shower her with gifts, maybe we'll start to carry ourselves well. At the best maybe she'll even make a knot in her throat. What I don't want to do is to throw the house out the window. In any case, I've been breaking my head to try to find the perfect gifts. I don't want to leave a stone to move. In the case of Tom, I know him like the palm of my hand but I simply don't know what she likes. I really like that sweater over there.
Déborah:	But it's just not of fashion. It goes with the flow and besides it looks like trash. But for tastes colors have been made. At least, I'm sure it would remain well.
Chelita:	The only thing I want is to find something of first.
Déborah:	There's that squinty saleswoman. She spends life ferociously. She always gets in my way.
Chelita:	I wonder if she lifts the elbow. Look at that dress over there; it's beautiful! If I'm nice to her maybe she'll give it to me at half price.
Déborah:	How foolish you are! You're in the clouds!
Chelita:	You're right. You know what? I'll just buy the presents next week when I have more energy. It's worth more late than never.

VOCABULARY

a fin de *exp.* in order to • (lit); to end of.

atravesársele a uno una persona *exp.* not to be able to stand someone • (lit); to have a person get in one's way.
SYNONYM: **no poder ver a uno ni en pintura** *exp.* not to be able to stand someone • (lit); not to be able to see someone not even in painting (as just their mere image would be too much to bear).

bizco(a) *adj.* cross-eyed • (lit); squint-eyed.
SYNONYM: **tener un ojo aquí y el otro en Pekín** *exp.* to be cross-eyed • (lit); to have an eye here and the other in Peking.

colmar a uno de *exp.* to shower someone with • (lit); to fill someone to the brim with.

conocer como la palma de la mano *exp.* to know backwards and forwards • (lit); to know like the palm of the hand.
SYNONYM (1): **saber de memoria** *exp.* • (lit); to know by memory, to know by heart (refers only to things, not to people).
SYNONYM (2): **saber al dedillo** *exp.* • (lit); to know like a finger • NOTE: This expression applies only to things, not to people.

corriente *adj.* ordinary, run-of-the-mill • (lit); (of the) current or flow.
SYNONYM: **ser del montón** *exp.* • (lit); to be of the heap or pile.

de primera *exp.* first-rate, the best • (lit); of first.

echar/tirar la casa por la ventana *exp.* to go overboard • (lit); to throw the house out the window.
ALSO: **sentirse como en casa** *exp.* to feel right at home • (lit); to feel like in home.

empinar el codo *exp.* • (lit); to raise the elbow.
SYNONYM: **chupar la botella** *exp.* • (lit); to suck the bottle.

estar bravo(a) *exp.* **1.** to be ill-tempered • **2.** (Chile) hot, highly seasoned • **3.** (Cuba) angry • (lit); fierce, ferocious.
SYNONYM (1): **levantarse del pie izquierdo** *exp.* to get up on the wrong side of the bed • (lit); to get up on the left foot.

estar de moda *exp.* to be fashionable, to be chic • (lit); to be of fashion.
SYNONYM: **de buen tono** *exp.* • (lit); of good tone.

estar en las nubes *exp.* to be daydreaming • (lit); to be in the clouds.
SYNONYM: **estar soñando** *adj.* • (lit); to be in a dreamlike state • NOTE: This comes from the verb *soñar* meaning "to dream."

hacérsele a uno un nudo en la garganta *exp.* to get a lump in one's throat • (lit); to have a knot form in one's throat.
ALSO: **tener buena garganta** *exp.* to have a good voice • (lit); to have (a) good throat • NOTE: This could best be compared to the expression "to have a golden throat."

la niña de sus ojos *exp.* the apple of one's eye, darling, treasure • (lit); the little girl of one's eyes.
NOTE: **niña del ojo** *exp.* pupil (of the eye).
ALSO: **¡mucho ojo!** *exp.* Watch out! Be careful! • (lit); much eye • NOTE: This expression is commonly shortened simply to *¡Ojo!* Watch out!

llevarse bien/mal con *exp.* to get/not to get along well with • (lit); to carry oneself off well/badly with.
ALSO: **hacer buenas migas** *exp.* to hit it off • (lit); to make good crumbs (together).

llevarse como perro y gato *exp.* to fight like cat and dog • (lit); to carry each other like dog and cat • NOTE: This is always used in reference to two or more people.
SEE: **llevarse bien/mal**

más vale tarde que nunca *exp.* better late than never • (lit); it is worth more late than never.

matar dos pájaros de un tiro *exp.* to kill two birds with one stone • (lit); to kill two birds with one throw.

no dejar piedra por mover *exp.* to leave no stone unturned • (lit); not to leave a stone to be moved.

quedarle bien *exp.* to fit someone well, to be becoming (on someone) • (lit); to remain well (on someone).

romperse/calentarse la cabeza *exp.* to rack one's brains • (lit); to break/heat up one's head.
SYNONYM: **romperse/calentarse los cascos** *exp.* • (lit); to break/to heat up one's skull.

ser bobo(a) *adj.* to be silly, stupid, foolish. • (lit); to be naive, simple.

ser de pacotilla *exp.* to be worthless junk • (lit); to be trash.

SYNONYM (1): **no valer un comino** *exp.* • (lit); not to be worth a cumin.

SYNONYM (2): **no valer un cacahuete** *exp.* (Mexico) • (lit); not to be worth a peanut.

SYNONYM (3): **no valer un cacao** *exp.* (Central America) • (lit); not to be worth a cocoa bean.

SYNONYM (4): **no valer un palo de tabaco** *exp.* (Colombia) • (lit); not to be worth a stick of tobacco.

SYNONYM (5): **no valer un taco** *exp.* (Colombia) • (lit); not to be worth a taco.

SYNONYM (6): **estar para el gato** *exp.* (Chile) • (lit); to be for the cat (or: something the cat dragged in).

PRACTICE THE VOCABULARY

[Answers to Lesson 13, p. 190]

A. Underline the appropriate word(s) that best complete(s) the sentence.

1. Vine a (**comienzo, fin**) de buscar un regalo para mi novio.

2. Más vale (**tarta, tarde**) que nunca.

3. Para gustos se han hecho (**colores, números**).

4. Lo único que quiero es encontrar algo de (**primera, segunda**).

5. Lo que no quiero hacer es echar la (**casca, casa**) por la ventana.

6. Me he estado rompiendo la (**casa, cabeza**) tratando de encontrar los regalos perfectos.

7. Lo conozco como la palma de mi (**brazo, mano**).

8. Me pregunto si empina el (**codo, pie**).

9. No quiero dejar (**piedra, piedad**) por mover.

10. A lo mejor hasta se le hace un (**nudillo, nudo**) en la garganta.

11. Allí está esa vendedora (**biznieta, bizca**).

12. Es el cumpleaños de mi futura suegra y así mato dos (**pájaros, pajareras**) de un tiro.

B. Choose the appropriate words below that complete the following expressions.

ventana	palma	llevarse
colmar	niña	moda
corriente	pacotilla	bobo
atravesársele	quedarle	fin

1. _____ **bien** *exp.* to fit someone well

2. **echar/tirar la casa por la** _____ *exp.* to go overboard

3. **a** _____ **de** *exp.* in order to

4. **conocer como la** _____ **de la mano** *exp.* to know backwards and forwards, like the palm of one's hand

5. **ser** _____ *adj.* to be silly

6. **estar de** _____ *exp.* to be fashionable, to be chic

7. **la** _____ **de sus ojos** *exp.* the apple of one's eye

8. _____ *adj.* ordinary, run-of-the-mill

9. **ser de** _____ *exp.* to be worthless junk

10. _____ **a uno de** *exp.* to shower someone with

11. _____ **a uno una persona** *exp.* not to be able to stand someone

12. _____ **bien/mal con** *exp.* to get/not to get along well with

C. Find the words in the grid below using the word list from Exercise B on page 166.

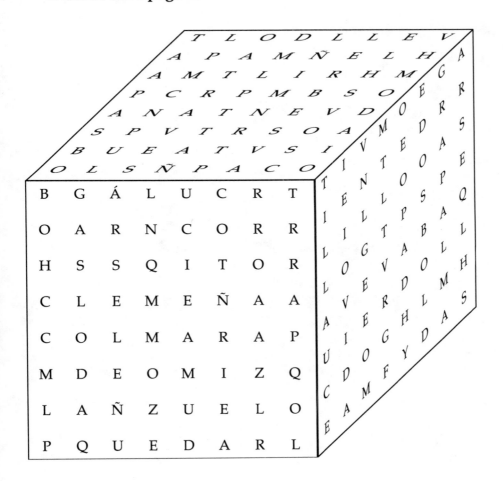

LESSON FOURTEEN

En la playa

(At the Beach)

¡Qué tiempo de perros!　　　　**¡Y tú estás de un humor de perros!**

EN LA PLAYA...

DIÁLOGO

Samuel y Donato están pasando el domingo en la playa.

Samuel:	¡Qué **tiempo de perros**!
Donato:	¡Y tú estás de un **humor de perros**!
Samuel:	Bueno, es que acabo de enterarme que Adela **se ha enredado con** Roberto.
Donato:	¿Desde cuándo?
Samuel:	Ya hace una semana. Y yo nunca me he **entendido bien con** él.
Donato:	Bueno, yo sé que hace tiempo que **se están echando el ojo** pero **a ver** lo que pasa. **Gústete o no**, se están viendo. ¡Él es tan **pesado**!
Samuel:	**Eso lo sabe hasta el gato**. A veces me dan ganas de **romperle la cara**.
Donato:	¡Y **buen** mentiroso que es! ¿Sabías que él siempre **engaña a** sus novias?
Samuel:	Yo sé. A propósito, dicen **las malas lenguas** que ellos **empinan el codo** hasta **jalarse** todas las noches **a partir de** las once. **Es la comidilla del pueblo**. ¡A que por eso **están bien envueltos en carne**!
Donato:	Seguro que siempre **están crudos**. Yo tendría que **guardar cama** al día siguiente. Probablemente me pasaría el día **echando las tripas**.

AT THE BEACH...

DIALOGUE

Samuel and Donato are spending Sunday at the beach.

Samuel: What lousy weather!

Donato: And you're in a lousy mood!

Samuel: Well, it's that I just I heard that Adela is having an affair with Roberto.

Donato: Since when?

Samuel: As of last week. And I've never been able to get along with him.

Donato: Well, I know they've been eyeing each other for a long time but let's see what happens. Whether you like it or not, they're seeing each other. He's such a geek!

Samuel: That's sure common knowledge. Sometimes I feel like clobbering him.

Donato: And he's such a liar! Did you know he always deceives his girl friends?

Samuel: I know. By the way, rumor has it that they drink until they get bombed every night starting at 11:00. It's the talk of the town. I bet that's why they're both so fat.

Donato: I'm sure they're always hung over. I'd have to stay in bed the next day. I'd probably be throwing up my guts all day.

Literal Translation of Dialogue

DIALOGUE

Samuel and Donato are passing Sunday at the beach.

Samuel:	What weather of dogs!
Donato:	And you're in a disposition of dogs!
Samuel:	Well, it's that I just heard that Adela got herself entangled with Roberto.
Donato:	Since when?
Samuel:	It's already been a week. I've never understood myself well with him.
Donato:	Well, I know it's been a time that they've been throwing each other the eye but to see what happens. It pleases you or not, they're seeing each other. He's so heavy!
Samuel:	Even the cat knows that. At times I feel like breaking his face.
Donato:	And what a good liar he is! Did you know that he always deceives his girl friends?
Samuel:	I know. To purpose, the bad tongues say that they raise the elbow until they pull themselves every night from the leaving of 11:00. It's the food of the neighborhood. To that for that they are well-wrapped in flesh!
Donato:	I'm sure that they're always raw. I'd have to keep bed the next day. I'd probably spend the day throwing out guts.

VOCABULARY

a partir de *exp.* as of, beginning at • (lit); from the leaving of, from the setting off of.

a ver *exp.* let's see • (lit); to see.
  SYNONYM: **vamos a ver** *exp.* • (lit); let's go see.

buen(a) *exp.* considerable, one heck-of-a, a real • (lit); good • *Tengo un buen constipado;* I have one heck-of-a cold.

echar las tripas *exp.* to throw up one's guts • (lit); to throw guts/tripes.
  SYNONYM: **arrojar** *v.* to throw up • (lit); to throw.

echarle el ojo a algo/alguien *exp.* to make eyes at something/someone • (lit); to throw the eye at something/someone.
  SYNONYM (1): **hacerle ojos a alguien** *exp.* • (lit); to make eyes at someone.
  SYNONYM (2): **comerse con los ojos** *exp.* • (lit); to eat someone up with one's eyes.

empinar el codo *exp.* to drink, to tipple • (lit); to raise the elbow.

engañar a uno *exp.* to fool someone, to deceive someone, to cheat on someone • (lit); to deceive someone.

enredarse con alguien *exp.* to have an affair with someone • (lit); to become entangled with someone.
  SYNONYM (1): **aventura amorosa** *exp.* • (lit); amorous adventure.
  SYNONYM (2): **estar metido(a) con alguien** *exp.* • (lit); to be placed with someone.

entenderse bien con alguien *exp.* to get along with someone • (lit); to understand each other well.
  SYNONYM: **llevarse bien con alguien** • (lit); to carry oneself well with someone.

eso lo sabe hasta el gato *exp.* everyone knows that, that's common knowledge • (lit); even the cat knows that.

estar bien envuelto(a) en carne *exp.* to be plump, to be fat • (lit); to be well-wrapped in flesh.
  ALSO: **en carne viva** *exp.* raw, without skin • (lit); in live flesh.

estar crudo(a) *exp.* (Mexico) to have a hangover • (lit); to be raw • ALSO: **tener una cruda** *exp.*
SYNONYM (1): **tener resaca** *exp.* (Eastern Argentina, Uruguay) • (lit); to have undertow.
SYNONYM (2): **tener un ratón** *exp.* (Venezuela, Colombia, Ecuador, Peru, Bolivia) • (lit); to have a mouse • ALSO: **estar enratonado(a)** *exp.* • (lit); to be "moused."
SYNONYM (3): **tener la mona** *exp.* (Chile) • (lit); to have the monkey.
SYNONYM (4): **estar de goma** *exp.* (Central America) • (lit); to be of rubber.

estar de humor de perros *exp.* to be in a lousy mood • (lit); to be in the mood of dogs.
SYNONYM: **tener malas pulgas**.
NOTE: The expression *de perros* meaning "lousy" can be used to modify other nouns as well. A variation of *de perros* is *perro(a)*. For example, *Pasé una noche perra;* I had a hell of a night.
ALSO (1): **a otro perro con ese hueso** *exp.* don't give me that baloney, get out of here, come off it • (lit); to another dog with that bone.
ALSO (2): **perro viejo** *exp.* cunning and experienced individual, sly old dog • (lit); old dog.

guardar cama *exp.* to stay in bed, to be confined to bed • (lit); to keep bed.

gústete o no *exp.* whether you like it or not • (lit); like it or not.

jalarse *v.* to get drunk • (lit); to pull oneself.
ALSO: **jalado(a)** *adj.* drunk, bombed, plastered.
SYNONYM (1): **pedo** *adj.* (Mexico) drunk, bombed • (lit); fart.
SYNONYM (2): **cuete** *adj.* (Mexico) drunk, bombed.
SYNONYM (3): **tomado** *adj.* (Cuba, Puerto Rico, Dominican Republic) drunk, bombed.
SYNONYM (4): **mamado** *adj.* (Eastern Argentina, Uruguay) drunk, bombed.
SYNONYM (5): **bolo** *adj.* (Central America) drunk, bombed.
SYNONYM (6): **chufifo** *adj.* (Chile) drunk, bombed.

las malas lenguas *exp.* rumor has it • (lit); the bad (or evil) tongues.
SYNONYM (1): **corre la voz que** *exp.* • (lit); the voice runs that.
SYNONYM (2): **corre la bola** *exp.* • (lit); the ball runs.

romperle a alguien la cara *exp.* to punch someone in the nose, to smash someone's face in • (lit); to break someone's face.
SYNONYM: **caerle a puñetazos a alguien** *exp.* • (lit); to have someone fall with punches.

ser la comidilla del pueblo *exp.* to be the talk of the town • (lit); to be the little food of the town.
SYNONYM: **andar en boca de todos** *exp.* everyone's talking about it • (lit); to go about in everyone's mouth.

ser pesado(a) *adj.* to be boring, dull, unpleasant • (lit); to be heavy.

tiempo de perros *exp.* lousy weather • (lit); weather of dogs.
   ALSO: **vida de perro** *exp.* a hard life • (lit); a dog's life.

PRACTICE THE VOCABULARY

[Answers to Lesson 14, p. 191]

A. Underline the correct definition.

1. **estar bien envuelto en carne:**
   a. to be thin   b. to be plump   c. to be sick

2. **echarle el ojo a alguien:**
   a. to be angry   b. to eye someone   c. to scream

3. **empinar el codo:**
   a. to drink heavily   b. to eat a lot   c. to diet

4. **estar crudo:**
   a. to be rude   b. to be well-mannered   c. to be hung over

5. **ser pesado:**
   a. to weigh a lot   b. to be thin   c. to be dull

6. **jalarse:**
   a. to get drunk   b. to sober up   c. to eat a lot

7. **humor de perros:**
   a. good mood   b. lousy mood   c. depressed

8. **la comidilla del pueblo:**
   a. dinner   b. the talk of the town   c. lunch

9. **echar las tripas:**
   a. to throw a fit   b. to throw up   c. to give up

10. **tiempo de perros:**
    a. lousy weather   b. beautiful weather   c. a good time

B. Match the columns.

☐ 1. Whether you like it or not, they're seeing each other.

☐ 2. I heard that Adela is having an affair with Roberto.

☐ 3. I'm sure they're always hung over.

☐ 4. You're in a lousy mood!

☐ 5. It's the talk of the town.

☐ 6. I'd be spending the day throwing my guts up.

☐ 7. That's common knowledge.

☐ 8. Sometimes I feel like clobbering him.

☐ 9. Rumor has it that they drink every night.

☐ 10. He's such a geek!

☐ 11. What lousy weather!

☐ 12. I've never been able to get along with him.

A. **¡Qué tiempo de perros!**

B. **Es la comidilla del pueblo.**

C. **Eso lo sabe hasta el gato.**

D. **Me pasaría el día echando las tripas.**

E. **Me enteré que Adela se ha enredado con Roberto.**

F. **¡Él es tan pesado!**

G. **Dicen las malas lenguas que empinan el codo todas las noches.**

H. **Gústete o no, se están viendo.**

I. **A veces me dan ganas de romperle la cara.**

J. **¡Tú estás de un humor de perros!**

K. **Yo nunca me he entendido bien con él.**

L. **Seguro que siempre están crudos.**

C. Fill in the blanks with the appropriate words from the list below that complete the expressions on page 177.

envuelto	comidilla	codo
engañar	tripas	cama
partir	jalarse	entenderse
enredarse	ver	cara

1. a _____ *exp.* let's see

2. _____ *v.* to get drunk

3. **estar bien** _____ **en carne** *exp.* to be plump, to be fat

4. **a** _____ **de** *exp.* as of, beginning on

5. **romperle a alguien la** _____ *exp.* to punch someone in the nose, to smash someone's face in

6. _____ **con alguien** *exp.* to have an affair with

7. **guardar** _____ *exp.* to stay in bed, to be confined to bed

8. **echar las** _____ *exp.* to throw up one's guts

9. _____ **bien con alguien** *exp.* to be on good terms with someone

10. **empinar el** _____ *exp.* to drink, to tipple

11. **ser la** _____ **del pueblo** *exp.* to be the talk of the town

12. _____ **a uno** *exp.* to cheat on someone

En la feria

(At the Carnival)

*Siento haber llegado tarde pero se me
descompuso el auto cuando venía para acá.
Después se me reventó una llanta. ¡Que lata!*

EN LA FERIA...

DIÁLOGO

Essie y Magda están en camino a la feria.

Essie: Siento haber llegado tarde pero **se me descompuso** el **auto** cuando venía para acá. Después se me reventó una llanta. **¡Qué lata!** No había contado con tantas demoras. ¡Creí que iba a **romper a llorar**! No creo que yo haya **nacido de pie**. De todos modos, logré arreglarla. **Por lo menos**, **me defiendo** en cuanto a lo mecánico. Mi madre dice que soy **aprendiza de todo, maestra de nada**.

Magda: Cuando uno está apurado, algo pasa **sin falta**. Sólo espero que no lleguemos demasiado tarde. ¡Está **muy allá**! Hace tanto tiempo que tengo deseos de ir.

Essie: No te preocupes que **estamos en las mismas**. Llegaremos con tiempo de sobra si nos vamos **ahorita**.

Magda: Probablemente debiésemos parar a comer algo **a la carrera**.

Essie: A este paso, no vamos a llegar nunca. Quisiera poder **correr** pero todo el mundo está andando **a paso de tortuga**.

Magda: El año pasado la feria estuvo **brutal**. Estaba repleta de **chamacos** que se **reían a carcajadas**.

AT THE CARNIVAL...

DIALOGUE

Essie and Magda are on their way to the carnival.

Essie: I'm sorry I arrived late but my car broke down on the way over here. Then I got a flat. What a drag! I wasn't counting on so many delays. I thought I was going to burst out crying! I don't think I was born lucky. Anyway, I managed to fix it. At least I get by when it comes to mechanical things. My mother says that I'm a jack of all trades, master of none.

Magda: Whenever you're in a hurry, something happens without fail. I just hope we don't get there too late. It's so far! I've been wanting to go there for such a long time.

Essie: Don't worry because we're all in the same boat. We'll get there in plenty of time if we leave right away.

Magda: We should probably stop and eat something on the run.

Essie: At this rate we'll never get there. I wish I could drive faster but everyone's moving at a snail's pace.

Magda: Last year the carnival was great. It was full of kids who were laughing hysterically.

Literal Translation of Dialogue

DIALOGUE

Essie and Magda are en route to the fair.

Essie: I'm sorry to have arrived late but my car decomposed when I came by here. Then my tire burst. What a tin plate! I hadn't counted on so many delays. I believed I was going to break to cry! I don't believe I was born on foot. Of all modes, I managed to fix it. For the least ones, I defend myself in when to the mechanics. My mother says that I'm an apprentice of everything, master of nothing.

Magda: When you're hurried, something happens without fail. I only hope we don't arrive too late. It's very over there! It's been so much time since I'd had desires to go.

Essie: Don't preoccupy yourself since we're in the same ones. We'll arrive with time of excess if we leave right now.

Magda: We should probably stop to eat something on the run.

Essie: At this pace, we're never going to arrive. I wish I could run but the whole world is moving at the pace of a turtle.

Magda: Last year the fair was brutal. It was full of kids who were laughing to guffaws.

VOCABULARY

a la carrera *exp.* on the run, hastily, hurriedly • NOTE: This comes from the verb *correr*, meaning "to run."

a paso de tortuga *exp.* at a snail's pace • (lit); at the pace of a turtle.

ahorita *adv.* **1.** (Mexico) at once, right now • **2.** (Cuba) in a moment • NOTE: Derived from the adverb *ahora* meaning "right now," *ahorita* is a common response made by waiters and waitresses when asked when the food will be arriving. This usage of *ahorita* is extremely popular in Latin America.
SYNONYM (1): **antualito** *adv.* (Colombia) • NOTE: This is a transformation of the adverb *antes* and means "right now."
SYNONYM (2): **al tiro** *exp.* (Chile) • (lit); to the throw.

aprendiz(za) de todo, maestro(a) de nada *exp.* jack of all trades, master of none • (lit); apprentice of all, master of nothing.

auto *m.* (especially Argentina, Chile, Uruguay) This is an abbreviation of *automóvil* meaning "car."
SYNONYM (1): **coche** *m.* (Spain, Mexico, Argentina, Uruguay) • (lit); coach, carriage • NOTE: In Guatemala, the masculine noun *coche* is commonly used to refer to "pork," and is a shortened form of the masculine noun "*cochino.*"
SYNONYM (2): **carro** *m.* (Guatemala, Peru, Cuba, Puerto Rico, Dominican Republic, Mexico) • (lit); cart, wagon • NOTE: In these countries, the feminine noun *carreta* would be used to indicate a "cart or wagon."

brutal *adj.* (especially Latin America) terrific, fantastic, incredible • *una película brutal;* a terrific film • (lit); brutal • NOTE: It is common to see a store sign with the words *Liquidación Brutal* meaning "Incredible Sale."
SYNONYM (1): **bárbaro** *adj.* (Spain) **1.** terrific • **2.** terrible • (lit); barbaric • NOTE: The differences in meaning simply depend on the tone of the speaker.
SYNONYM (2): **chévere** *adj.* (Cuba, Puerto Rico, Dominican Republic) This adjective supposedly originated from a Cuban song title.
SYNONYM (3): **lo máximo** *adj.* (Mexico) the ultimate • (lit); the maximum.

correr *v.* **1.** to drive fast, to speed • **2.** to hurry • *¡Corre! ¡Corre!* Hurry up! **3.** to fly (said of time) • *¡Cómo corre el tiempo!* How time flies! • (lit); to run.
SYNONYM: **fletado(a)** *adj.* (Venezuela, Colombia) quickly • NOTE: This comes from the verb *fletar*, meaning "to load freight."

chamaco(a) *n.* (Mexico) little boy/girl.
SYNONYM (1): **chaval(la)** *n.* (Spain) young man/woman, adolescent • ALSO: **chavalería** *f.* kids.
SYNONYM (2): **pibe** *n.* (Argentina and Uruguay).
SYNONYM (3): **patojo(a)** *n.* (Guatemala).
SYNONYM (4): **nene** *n.* (Argentina, Uruguay, Spain).
SYNONYM (5): **guambito** *n.* (Colombia).
SYNONYM (6): **cipote** *m.* (El Salvador).
SYNONYM (7): **pelado** *m.* (Colombia).
SYNONYM (8): **cabro** *m.* (Chile).
SYNONYM (9): **guagua** *f.* (Peru, Chile, Ecuador) baby • NOTE: This is an onomatopoeia since *guagua* is the type of sound a baby makes when crying. Although *guagua* is always feminine, it may equally be used to refer to a male baby. It is important to note than in Cuba and the Canary Islands, *guagua* means "municipal bus."

defenderse *v.* to get along, not to do badly, to be able to handle (a particular task) • (lit); to defend oneself.

descomponerse *v.* to break down (said of a car) • (lit); to decompose.
SYNONYM (1): **accidentado(a)** *adj.* 1. (Venezuela) broken-down (applied to a car) • 2. bumpy (applied to a road) • (lit); uneven (applied to roads).
SYNONYM (2): **estar descompuesto(a)** *adj.* (Mexico) • (lit); to be decomposed • *un motor descompuesto;* a broken-down motor.
SYNONYM (3): **tener una avería** *exp.* (Spain) • (lit); to have injuries • *El coche tiene una avería;* There is a problem with the car.
SYNONYM (4): **tener un pane/una pana** *exp.* (Peru, Ecuador).
SYNONYM (5): **una descompostura** *v.* (Mexico) This comes from the verb *descomponer* meaning "to break down." • NOTE: **composturas** *f.pl.* (Mexico) car repairs.
SYNONYM (6): **roto(a)** *adj.* (Cuba).

estar en las mismas *exp.* to be in the same boat • (lit); to be in the same (ones).

muy allá *exp.* miles away, much further on • (lit); very there.
NOTE: This is generally a very popular idiomatic expression.

nacer de pie *exp.* to be born lucky • (lit); to be born (on foot) standing
SYNONYM (1): **nacer parado(a)** *exp.* • (lit); to be born standing.
SYNONYM (2): **nacer con estrella** *exp.* to be born under a lucky star • (lit); to be born with star.

¡Qué lata! *exp.* What a drag! What a nuisance! What a bore! • (lit); What a tin can!

reír a carcajadas *exp.* to laugh uproariously • (lit); to laugh at guffaws.
  ALSO (1): **soltar una carcajada** *exp.* to guffaw, to burst out laughing • (lit); to release a guffaw.
  ALSO (2): **una buena carcajada** *exp.* a hearty laugh • (lit); a good guffaw.

romper a *exp.* • (lit); to break (out) in.
  SYNONYM: **echarse a** *exp.* to begin to, to burst out, to suddenly start to • (lit); to throw oneself to • *echarse a reír/llorar;* to burst out laughing/crying.

sin falta *exp.* without fail • (lit); without fault.

PRACTICE THE VOCABULARY

[Answers to Lesson 15, p. 192]

A. Match the two columns.

☐ 1. My car broke down.

☐ 2. It was full of kids who were laughing hysterically.

☐ 3. What a drag!

☐ 4. Don't worry because we're in the same boat.

☐ 5. I wish I could drive faster.

☐ 6. The carnival was great.

☐ 7. Jack of all trades, master of none.

☐ 8. We'll get there in plenty of time if we leave right away.

☐ 9. I though I was going to burst out crying.

A. **La feria estuvo brutal.**

B. **Creí que iba a romper a llorar.**

C. **¡Qué lata!**

D. **Quisiera poder correr.**

E. **Estaba llena de chamacos que se reían a carcajadas.**

F. **Llegaremos con tiempo de sobra si nos vamos ahorita.**

G. **Aprendiz de todo, maestro de nada.**

H. **No te preocupes que estamos en las mismas.**

I. **Se me descompuso el auto.**

B. Fill in the blanks with the correct words from the list below that best complete the expressions.

romper	lata	brutal
carrera	pie	correr
chamaco	ahorita	defenderse
descomponerse	aprendiz	falta

1. _____ adj. (especially Latin America) terrific, fantastic, incredible

2. _____ m. (Mexico) littly boy

3. _____ adv. 1. (Mexico) at once, right now • 2. (Cuba) in a moment

4. a la _____ exp. on the run, hastily, hurriedly

5. _____ v. to get along, not to do badly, to be able to handle (a particular task)

6. _____ v. to break down (said of a car)

7. nacer de _____ exp. to be born lucky

8. _____ v. 1. to drive fast, to speed • 2. to hurry

9. ¡Qué _____ ! exp. What a drag! What a nuisance! What a bore!

10. _____ a exp. to break out in (tears, etc.)

11. _____ de todo, maestro de nada exp. jack of all trades, master of none

12. sin _____ exp. without fail

C. Choose the correct synonym for the word(s) on the left.

1. **chamaco:**   a. little car   b. little boy

2. **brutal:**   a. nasty   b. terrific

3. **defenderse:**   a. to get along   b. to get angry

4. **¡Qué lata!:**   a. What a drag!   b. How terrific!

5. **carcajada:**   a. big car   b. guffaw

6. **a la carrera:**   a. on the run   b. slowly

7. **nacer de pie:**   a. to be born lucky   b. to eat a lot

8. **correr:**   a. to leave   b. to drive fast

9. **muy allá:**   a. near   b. far

10. **ahorita:**   a. right now   b. later

ANSWERS TO LESSONS 11-15

LESSON ELEVEN - *El partido de fútbol*

Practice the Vocabulary

A. 1. a
   2. b
   3. b
   4. b
   5. b
   6. a
   7. b
   8. b
   9. b
   10. a
   11. a
   12. b

B. 1. ilusiones
   2. verme
   3. punto
   4. buenas
   5. canta un gallo
   6. en cuando
   7. paso
   8. vista
   9. gota
   10. lija
   11. punta
   12. suena

C. 1. E
   2. H
   3. K
   4. D
   5. I
   6. C
   7. J
   8. L
   9. A
   10. F
   11. B
   12. G

D. **Answers to CROSSWORD PUZZLE.**

									⁴V	
	¹V	²I	S	T	A		³V	E	R
		L						R	
	⁵S	U						D	
	O	S			⁶N		A	
	N	I		⁷P	A	R	A	D	O
⁸P	A	S	O		R				
	R	⁹N	A	R	I	C	E	S	
	L	E			Z				
	E	S			Ó				
		¹⁰P	U	N	T	O			

LESSON TWELVE - *El cine*

Practice the Vocabulary

A. 1. cuervos
   2. coba
   3. tema
   4. mismo
   5. chino
   6. culata
   7. revienta
   8. duro
   9. caballos
   10. genio
   11. estilo
   12. chivo

B. 1. b   7. b
    2. a   8. a
    3. a   9. b
    4. b   10. b
    5. b   11. b
    6. a   12. b

C. 1. H   7. I
    2. K   8. G
    3. F   9. C
    4. D   10. J
    5. E   11. L
    6. B   12. A

LESSON THIRTEEN - *En el rastro*

Practice the Vocabulary

A. 1. fin   7. mano
    2. tarde   8. codo
    3. colores   9. piedra
    4. primera   10. nudo
    5. casa   11. bizca
    6. cabeza   12. pájaros

B. 1. quedarle   7. niña
    2. ventana   8. corriente
    3. izquierdo   9. pacotilla
    4. palma   10. colmar
    5. bobo   11. atravesársele
    6. moda   12. fin

C. **Answers to WORD GRID.**

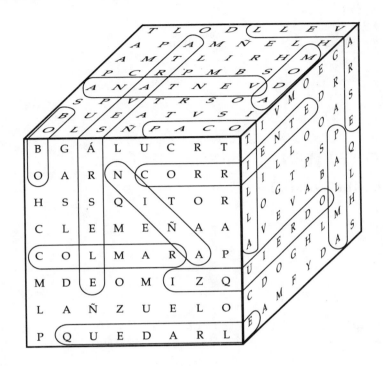

LESSON FOURTEEN - *En la playa*

Practice the Vocabulary

A. 1. b
   2. b
   3. a
   4. c
   5. c

   6. a
   7. b
   8. b
   9. b
   10. a

B. 1. H
   2. E
   3. L
   4. J
   5. B
   6. D

   7. C
   8. I
   9. G
   10. F
   11. A
   12. K

C. 1. ver
    2. jalarse
    3. envuelto
    4. partir
    5. cara
    6. enredarse

    7. cama
    8. tripas
    9. entenderse
    10. codo
    11. comidilla
    12. engañar

LESSON FIFTEEN - *En la feria*

Practice the Vocabulary

A. 1. I
    2. E
    3. C
    4. H
    5. D

    6. A
    7. G
    8. F
    9. B

B. 1. brutal
    2. chamaco
    3. ahorita
    4. carrera
    5. defenderse
    6. descomponerse

    7. pie
    8. correr
    9. lata
    10. romper
    11. aprendiz
    12. falta

C. 1. b
    2. b
    3. a
    4. a
    5. b

    6. a
    7. a
    8. b
    9. b
    10. a

REVIEW EXAM FOR LESSONS 11-15

[Answers to Review, p. 197]

A. Underline the correct translation of the expression in bold.

1. **ahorita:**
   a. far away
   b. right away

2. **nacer de pie:**
   a. to be born rich
   b. to be born lucky

3. **a la carrera:**
   a. slowly
   b. on the run

4. **jalarse:**
   a. to get drunk
   b. to become angry

5. **echar las tripas:**
   a. to throw up
   b. to give up

6. **saltar a la vista:**
   a. to fly off the handle
   b. to be obvious

7. **estar bien envuelto en carne:**
   a. to be plump
   b. to be thin

8. **enredarse con alguien:**
   a. to have a fight with someone
   b. to have an affair with someone

9. **empinar el codo:**
   a. to drink heavily
   b. to get into a fist fight

10. **estar crudo:**
    a. to have a hangover
    b. to be drunk

B. Choose the word that best completes the phrase.

colores	ventana	nunca
codo	gato	enredado
ahorita	lata	romper
perros	allá	pie
descompuso	brutal	defiendo

1. Lo que no quiero hacer es echar la casa por la _____ .

2. Para gustos se han hecho _____ .

3. Me pregunto si empina el _____ .

4. Más vale tarde que _____ .

5. ¡Qué tiempo de _____ !

6. Me enteré que Adela se ha _____ con Roberto.

7. Eso lo sabe hasta el _____ .

8. Siento haber llegado tarde pero se me _____ el auto.

9. Me _____ en cuanto a lo mecánico.

10. Espero que no lleguemos demasiado tarde. Está muy _____ .

11. El año pasado la feria estuvo _____ .

12. No creo que yo haya nacido de _____ .

13. Llegaremos con tiempo de sobra si nos vamos _____ .

14. Se me reventó una llanta. ¡Qué _____ !

15. Creí que iba a _____ a llorar.

C. Find the words used in the list for Exercise B in the grid below.

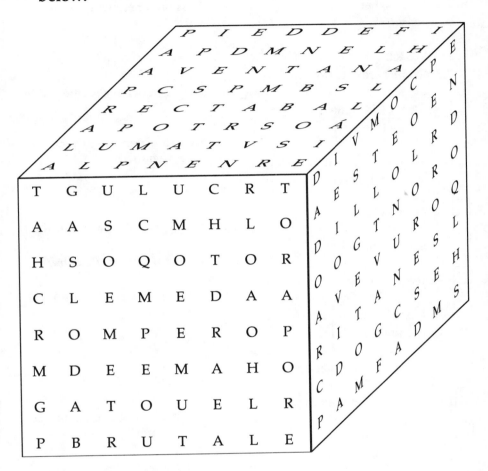

D. Match the two columns.

☐ 1. Hey, what are you doing here?

☐ 2. To tell you the truth, I only come here occasionally.

☐ 3. I have his name on the tip of my tongue.

☐ 4. Last time I saw him, he fell right on his face.

☐ 5. No way!

☐ 6. To each his own.

☐ 7. It's getting dark.

☐ 8. It bothers me to have to spend so much money.

☐ 9. I'll try to butter her up.

☐ 10. You're out of your mind!

☐ 11. It's a neat movie and worth going.

☐ 12. I thought you two didn't get along.

☐ 13. It's not in style.

☐ 14. I wonder if she takes a nip or two on the job.

☐ 15. It's really run-of-the-mill and looks cheap besides.

A. **Me revienta tener que gastar tanto dinero.**

B. **Cada loco con su tema.**

C. **Es una película chévere y vale la pena ir.**

D. **La última vez que lo vi se cayó de narices.**

E. **¡Qué va!**

F. **Vaya, ¿y tú qué haces aquí?**

G. **Voy a tratar de darle coba.**

H. **Me pregunto si ella empina el codo en el trabajo.**

I. **No está de moda.**

J. **Se está haciendo noche.**

K. **Tengo su nombre en la punta de la lengua.**

L. **Yo creía que ustedes se llevaban como perro y gato.**

M. **A decir verdad, vengo solamente de cuando en cuando.**

N. **Se ve muy corriente y además parece ser de pacotilla.**

O. **¡Tú estás más loco que un chivo!**

ANSWERS TO REVIEW EXAM FOR LESSONS 11-15

A.
1. b
2. b
3. b
4. a
5. a
6. b
7. a
8. b
9. a
10. a

B.
1. ventana
2. colores
3. codo
4. nunca
5. perros
6. enredado
7. gato
8. descompuso
9. defiendo
10. allá
11. brutal
12. pie
13. ahorita
14. lata
15. romper

C. **Answers to WORD GAME.**

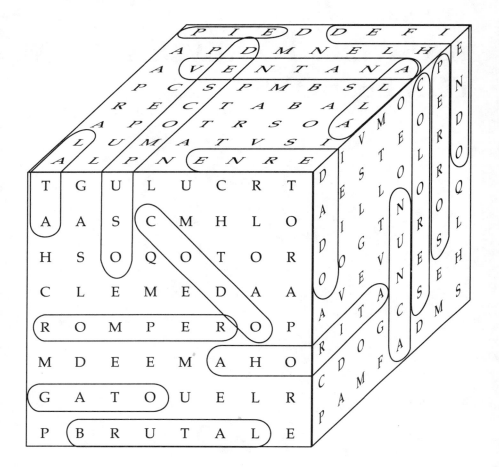

D. 1. F   9. G
    2. M   10. O
    3. K   11. C
    4. D   12. L
    5. E   13. I
    6. B   14. H
    7. J   15. N
    8. A

Being Obscene Unintentionally

(and other embarrassing moments)

BEING OBSCENE UNINTENTIONALLY
(and other embarrassing moments)

Americans naturally assume that when they go to another English-speaking country like England, for example, they will certainly have no problem communicating and will be readily understood. However, the unsuspecting traveler learns quickly that this is *not* the case.

As an American, if you ask a hotel or innkeeper where the restroom is, you'll undoubtedly evoke a confused response of, "But sir, you're standing in it!" Hmmm. Looks like an awfully fancy bathroom. Perhaps he didn't quite understand. No problem. Simply rephrase the question and ask for the bathroom. "Oh! Yes, of course, sir! Just down that corridor." Finally! You've made yourself understood… or have you? When you open the door to the bathroom and all you see is just that, a bath, you'll quickly realize that something is wrong because in England the bathroom is referred to as the toilet and the bath is in a separate room altogether, the bathroom.

In Spanish, the speaker has to be concerned with 20 different Spanish-speaking countries, which dramatically increases the chance for innocent blunders of this sort.

In this section, you'll see a sentence in Spanish followed by the different possible translations that it can have depending on context or country.

Once you've studied the following list, you'll begin to see that if a native of Spain asks a native of Argentina where to catch the bus, the Argentinian may stand there stunned for a moment, then run away!

¿Dónde puedo coger el autobús?

Common Translation:
> Where can I catch the bus?

Translation in Argentina / Chile / Mexico:
> Where can I fuck the bus?

NOTE: In Argentina and Chile, these are the preferred ways to say, "Where can I catch the bus?"

- ¿Dónde puedo agarrar *(to grab, to seize)* el autobús?
- ¿Dónde puedo tomar *(to take)* el autobús?
- ¿Dónde puedo pillar *(to catch)* el autobús?
- ¿Dónde puedo recoger *(to pick up, to gather, to fetch)* el autobús?

¿Quieres que te fría un huevo?

Common Translation #1:
> Would you like me to fry you an egg?

Common Translation #2:
> Would you like me to fry one of your balls?

¿Te gusta la papaya?

Common Translation:
> Do you like papaya?

Translation in Cuba / Puerto Rico / Dominican Republic:
> Do you like pussy (vagina)?

NOTE: In Cuba, *papaya* is referred to as *fruta bomba* or "puffed-out fruit."

¿Conoces a ese individuo?

Common Translation:
> Do you know that guy?

Translation in Argentina:
> Do you know that weird person?

NOTE: In Argentina, the masculine noun *individuo* should be used with caution since it is insulting.

Conozco a ese pájaro.

Translation in Chile / Peru / Ecuador:
> I know that guy.

Translation in Cuba / Puerto Rico / Dominican Republic:
> I know that faggot.

Voy a la playa a buscar almejas.

Common Translation #1:
> I go to the beach to look for clams.

Common Translation #2:
> I go to the beach to look for pussy (vagina) .

Cuando veo un bicho lo pisoteo.

Common Translation #1:
    Whenever I see a bug, I squash it.

Common Translation #2:
    Whenever I see a dick (penis) , I squash it.

Este restaurante tiene los mejores bollos.

Common Translation:
    This restaurant has the best bread rolls.

Translation in Cuba:
    This restaurant has the best pussy (vagina).

Voy a la playa a buscar conchas.

Common Translation:
    I go to the beach to look for seashells.

Translation in Mexico:
    I go to the beach to look for pussy (vagina).

Mi madre me va a comprar un conejo para mi cumpleaños.

Common Translation:
    My mother's going to buy me a rabbit for my birthday.

Translation in Mexico:
    My mother's going to buy me a pussy (vagina) for my birthday.

Me comí un chorizo entero a la hora del desayuno.

Common Translation #1:
    I ate a whole pork sausage for breakfast.

Common Translation #2:
    I ate a whole dick (penis) for breakfast.

¡Mira! Ese hombre está vendiendo churros.

Common Translation:
Look! That man's selling fritters.

Translation in Mexico:
Look! That man's selling dicks (penises)!

¡Qué follón tan horrible!

Common Translation:
What a horrible mess!

Translation in Mexico:
What a horrible fart!

Vamos a coger mariposas.

Common Translation:
We're going to catch butterflies.

Translation in Argentina / Chile / Mexico:
We're going to fuck faggots.

¡Esos melocotones son enormes!

Common Translation:
Those peaches are enormous!

Translation in Mexico:
Those boobs are enormous!

Creo que venden nabos en este mercado.

Common Translation #1:
I think they sell turnips in this market.

Common Translation #2:
I think they sell dicks (penises) in this market.

Le echó un palo a su perro.

Common Translation #1:
    He threw his dog a stick.

Common Translation #2:
    He fucked his dog.

NOTE: **echar un palo** *exp.* to screw, copulate with • (lit); to throw a stick.

¿Soplaste ese pito?

Common Translation #1:
    Did you blow that whistle?

Common Translation #2:
    Did you blow that dick (penis)?

El policía lo golpeó con su porra.

Common Translation:
    The policeman beat him with his club.

Translation in Mexico:
    The policeman beat him with his dick (penis) .

Sirvieron el biftec con una seta grande encima.

Common Translation:
    They served the steak with a big mushroom on top.

Translation in Mexico:
    They served the steak with a big pussy (vagina) on top.

Es mi tortillera favorita.

Common Translation #1:
    She's my favorite tortilla vendor.

Common Translation #2:
    She's my favorite dyke.

Esta sopa tiene muchos zurullos.

Common Translation #1:
This soup has a lot of lumps in it.

Common Translation #2:
This soup has a lot of turds in it.

¡Qué vista tan bella desde este pico!

Common Translation #1:
What a beautiful view from this peak!

Common Translation #2:
What a beautiful view from this dick (penis)!

Mi hermana cría pollas.

Common Translation #1:
My sister raises young hens.

Common Translation #2:
My sister raises dicks (penises).

Voy a la tienda a comprar una cajetilla.

Common Translation:
I'm going to the store to buy a pack of cigarettes.

Translation in Argentina / Uruguay:
I'm going to the store to buy a faggot.

Mi chucha acaba de parir.

Common Translation:
My female dog just had babies.

Translation in Chile:
My pussy (vagina) just had babies.

Mi padre me regaló un coche para mi cumpleaños.

Common Translation:
My father gave me a car for my birthday.

Translation in Guatemala:
My father gave me a pig for my birthday.

Estoy muy embarazada.

Mistaken Translation:
I'm very embarrassed.

Actual Translation:
I'm very pregnant.

GLOSSARY

The glossary contains all the slang, idioms, and expressions that were used in the dialogues.

-A-

a decir verdad *exp.* to tell (you) the truth • (lit); to say the truth.

a dos pasos de aquí *exp.* a few steps away, a short distance from here, nearby • (lit); two steps from here.

a espaldas de alguien *exp.* behind someone's back • (lit); to the back of someone.
ALSO (1): **echarse algo sobre las espaldas** *exp.* to bear a burden • (lit); to throw something on one's back.
ALSO (2): **tirar de espaldas a alguien** *exp.* to floor someone (with news) • (lit); to throw someone on his/her back • *Esta noticia me tiró de espaldas;* This piece of news just floored me.

a fin de *exp.* in order to • (lit); to end of.

a fondo *exp.* completely, thoroughly • (lit); to the bottom • *dormir a fondo;* to sleep deeply.
ALSO (1): **de fondo** *exp.* long-distance • (lit); of bottom • *corredor de fondo;* long-distance runner.
ALSO (2): **en el fondo** *exp.* deep down (within a person) • *En el fondo, es muy generoso;* Deep down, he's very generous.

a la carrera *exp.* on the run, hastily, hurriedly • NOTE: This comes from the verb *correr,* meaning "to run."

a la corta o a la larga *exp.* in the short or long run • (lit); in the short (run) or in the long (run).
SYNONYM: **a la larga** *exp.* in the long run • (lit); in the long.

a la hora *exp.* on time, punctually • (lit); on the hour • *Llegó a la hora;* He/She arrived on time.
ALSO: **a buena hora** *exp.* at an

opportune time • (lit); at good hour.

a las buenas/malas *exp.* willingly/unwillingly • (lit); in a good/bad way.
SYNONYM (1): **por las buenas/malas** *exp.* • (lit); for the good/bad ones.
SYNONYM (2): **por las buenas o por las malas** *exp.* whether one likes it or not • (lit); for the good or for the bad ones.
SYNONYM (3): **de mangas o de faldas** *exp.* (Ecuador) • (lit); from sleeves or from skirts.

a partir de *exp.* as of, beginning at • (lit); from the leaving of, from the setting off of.

a paso de tortuga *exp.* at a snail's pace • (lit); at the pace of a turtle.

a que *exp.* I'll bet (you) • (lit); to that.

a santo de qué *exp.* for what reason • (lit); to saint of what.
ALSO (1): **santo(a)** *adj.* blessed • (lit); holy • *Todo el santo día;* The whole blessed day.
ALSO (2): **desnudar a un santo para vestir a otro** *exp.* to rob Peter to pay Paul • (lit); to undress a saint to clothe another.

a toda prisa *exp.* at full speed, as quickly as possible • (lit); at all speed.
SYNONYM (1): **a toda vela** *exp.* under full sail, at full speed • (lit); at all sail.
SYNONYM (2): **en un avemaría** *exp.* in a jiffy • (lit); in one Hail Mary.

SYNONYM (3): **en un chiflido** *exp.* in a jiffy • (lit); in one whistle.
SYNONYM (4): **en un credo** *exp.* in a jiffy • (lit); in one creed.
SYNONYM (5): **en un decir Jesús** *exp.* in a jiffy• (lit); in one saying of Jesus.
SYNONYM (6): **en un dos por tres** *exp.* in a jiffy • (lit); in a two by three.
SYNONYM (7): **en un improviso** *exp.* (Colombia, Venezuela, Mexico) in a jiffy • (lit); in one sudden action.
SYNONYM (8): **en un salto** *exp.* in a jiffy • (lit); in one leap.
SYNONYM (9): **en un soplo** *exp.* in a jiffy • (lit); in a gust or blow.

a todas luces *exp.* any way you look at it, clearly • (lit); by all lights.
ALSO: **de pocas luces** *exp.* stupid, dim-witted • (lit); of little lights • NOTE: This could best be compared to the American expression, "The lights are on but nobody's home."
SYNONYM: **a toda luz** *exp.* • (lit); by all light.

a ver *exp.* let's see • (lit); to see.
SYNONYM: **vamos a ver** *exp.* • (lit); let's go see.

abrirse paso *exp.* to work one's way through (a crowd, etc.) • (lit); to open passage.

acabar de (+ infinitive) *exp.* to have just (+ past participle) • (lit); to finish.
SYNONYM (1): **venir de (+ infinitive)** *exp.* (Colombia) • (lit); to come to (+ infinitive).
SYNONYM (2): **recién (+ past**

participle) *exp.* (Eastern Argentina, Uruguay, Chile) • (lit); recent (+ past participle).

aflojar *v.* (Mexico, Cuba, Puerto Rico, Dominican Republic, Eastern Argentina, Uruguay) to fork out, to cough up • (lit); to loosen.
SYNONYM: **soltar** *v.* • (lit); to release.

ahogarse en un vaso de agua *exp.* to get all worked up about nothing, to make a mountain out of a molehill • (lit); to drown in a glass of water.
SYNONYM: **ahogarse en poca agua** *exp.* • (lit); to drown in a little water.
ALSO: **ahogar en germen** *exp.* to nip in the bud • (lit); to drown while it's still only a germ.

ahorita *adv.* 1. (Mexico) at once, right now • 2. (Cuba) in a moment • NOTE: Derived from the adverb *ahora* meaning "right now," *ahorita* is a common response made by waiters and waitresses when asked when the food will be arriving. This usage of *ahorita* is extremely popular in Latin America.
SYNONYM (1): **antualito** *adv.* (Colombia) • NOTE: This is a transformation of the adverb *antes* and means "right now."
SYNONYM (2): **al tiro** *exp.* (Chile) • (lit); to the throw.

al fin y al cabo *exp.* anyway, in the end, after all, when all is said and done • (lit); to the end and the end.

SYNONYM: **al fin y al fallo** *exp.* (Chile) • (lit); to the end and the judgment.

al primer golpe de vista *exp.* at first glance • (lit); at first stroke/blow/knock of sight.

andar en boca de todos *exp.* to have everyone talking about it, to be on everyone's lips • (lit); to go into everyone's mouth.
SYNONYM: **andar en boca de las gentes** *exp.* • (lit); to be in the mouth of the people.

andarse por las ramas *exp.* to beat around the bush • (lit); to stroll/walk by the branches.
SYNONYM: **andar con rodeos** *exp.* • (lit); to walk with detours.
NOTE: **emborrachar la perdiz** *exp.* (Chile) to beat around the bush • (lit); to get the partridge drunk.

aprendiz(za) de todo, maestro(a) de nada *exp.* jack of all trades, master of none • (lit); apprentice of all, master of nothing.

arreglárselas para *exp.* to manage to • (lit); to arrange oneself by.
ALSO: **¡Ya te arreglaré!** *exp.* I'll fix you!, I'll get even with you! • (lit); I'll arrange you!

atravesársele a uno una persona *exp.* not to be able to stand someone • (lit); to have a person get in one's way.
SYNONYM: **no poder ver a uno ni en pintura** *exp.* not to be able to stand someone • (lit); not to be able to see someone not even in painting (as just their mere image would be to much to bear).

auto *m.* (especially Argentina, Chile, Uruguay) This is an abbreviation of *automóvil* meaning "car."
SYNONYM (1): **coche** *m.* (Spain, Mexico, Argentina, Uruguay) • (lit); coach, carriage • NOTE: In Guatemala, the masculine noun *coche* is commonly used to refer to "pork," and is a shortened form of the masculine noun *"cochino."*
SYNONYM (2): **carro** *m.* (Guatemala, Peru, Cuba, Puerto Rico, Dominican Republic, Mexico) • (lit); cart, wagon • NOTE: In these countries, the feminine noun *carreta* would be used to indicate a "cart or wagon."

-B-

bizco(a) *adj.* cross-eyed • (lit); squint-eyed.
SYNONYM: **tener un ojo aquí y el otro en Pekín** *exp.* to be cross-eyed • (lit); to have an eye here and the other in Peking.

boca abajo *exp.* face down • (lit); mouth down.
ANTONYM: **boca arriba** *exp.* face up • (lit); mouth up.

brindar *exp.* to drink a toast • (lit); to drink in chorus.

brutal *adj.* (especially Latin America) terrific, fantastic, incredible • *una película brutal;* a terrific film • (lit); brutal • NOTE: It is common to see a store sign

with the words *Liquidación Brutal* meaning "Incredible Sale."
SYNONYM (1): **bárbaro** *adj.* (Spain) **1.** terrific • **2.** terrible • (lit); barbaric • NOTE: The differences in meaning simply depend on the tone of the speaker.
SYNONYM (2): **chévere** *adj.* (Cuba, Puerto Rico, Dominican Republic) This adjective supposedly originated from a Cuban song title.
SYNONYM (3): **lo máximo** *adj.* (Mexico) the ultimate • (lit); the maximum.

buen(a) *exp.* considerable, one heck-of-a, a real • (lit); good • *Tengo un buen constipado;* I have one heck-of-a cold.

buena gente *exp.* good egg, nice guy • (lit); good people.

bueno(a) *adj. & interj.* **1.** well... • **2.** fine! • **3.** bad, nasty • *un buen constipado;* a nasty cold • **4.** considerable • *una buena cantidad;* a considerable amount • **5.** come off it! • **6.** okay.

buscarle tres pies al gato *exp.* to go looking for trouble • (lit); to look for three of the cat's feet.
SYNONYM (1): **buscarle cinco pies al gato** *exp.* • (lit); to look for five of the cat's feet.
SYNONYM (2): **buscarle mangas al chaleco** *exp.* • (lit); to look for sleeves in the vest.
NOTE (1): **buscarle los tres pies al gato** *exp.* (Cuba) Note that in Cuba, the definite article *los* is used before *tres pies.*
NOTE (2): **buscarle cinco pies al**

gato *exp.* (Ecuador) to go looking for trouble • (lit); to search for a five-footed cat.

-C-

cabos sueltos *m.pl.* • (lit); loose ends.

cada loco con su tema *exp.* to each his own • (lit); each lunatic with his/her theme.
SYNONYM (1): **para gustos se han hecho colores** *exp.* • (lit); for tastes colors have been made.
SYNONYM (2): **cada perico a su estaca, cada chango a su mecate** *exp.* • (lit); each parakeet (or parrot) to his perch, each monkey to his cord.

caer de narices *exp.* to fall on one's face • (lit); to fall on one's nose.

cantar de plano *exp.* to make a full confession, to confess, to spill the beans • (lit); to sing straightforwardly.
NOTE: **de plano** *exp.* directly, straightforwardly.

cantarle las cuarenta *exp.* to tell someone off, to tell someone exactly what's what • (lit); to sing the forty (truths about the person).

cara a cara *exp.* **1.** right to a person's face • **2.** privately • (lit); face to face.
ALSO (1): **tener mucha cara** *exp.*to have a lot of nerve • (lit); to have a lot of face • *Ese tipo tiene mucha*

cara; That guy's got a lot of nerve • *No tengo cara para hacer algo;* I don't have the nerve to do that.
ALSO (2): **dar la cara** *exp.* to face up to things • (lit); to give face.
ALSO (3): **dar/sacar la cara por uno** *exp.* to stand up for someone, to defend someone • (lit); to give/to stick out the face for someone.
ALSO (4): **poner a mal tiempo buena cara** *exp.*to keep a stiff upper lip • (lit); to put good face in bad times.
ALSO (5): **poner buena cara a algo** *exp.*to take something well • (lit); to put good face to something.
ALSO (6): **tener cara de** *exp.* to look • (lit); to have face of • *Tener cara de tristeza;* To look sad.

cargar la mano *exp.* **1.** to overcharge • **2.** to crack down, to be too strict • **3.** to be heavy-handed with a certain ingredient in a recipe • (lit); to load the hand.
SYNONYM (1): **cargar la cuenta** *exp.* • (lit); to (over)charge the account.
SYNONYM (2): **pasársele la mano** *exp.* • (lit); to pass the hand • *Se le pasa la mano;* He overcharges him/her.

clavar los ojos en *exp.*: to stare at, to fix one's eyes on • (lit); to nail one's eyes on.
SYNONYM (1): **clavar la vista en** *exp.* • (lit); to nail the sight on.
SYNONYM (2): **clavar la atención en** *exp.* • (lit); to fix one's attention on.
SYNONYM (3): **guiñar un ojo** *exp.* to make eyes at, to flirt • (lit); to

wink (an eye).
SYNONYM (4): **hacer ojos** *exp.*
(Colombia) • (lit); to make eyes.
SYNONYM (5): **hacer ojitos** *exp.*
(Mexico) • (lit); to make little
eyes.
SYNONYM (6): **hacer caras** *exp.*
(Eastern Argentina, Uruguay) •
(lit); to make faces.

**coger a alguien con las manos en
la masa** *exp.* to catch someone in
the act, to catch someone
red-handed • (lit); to catch
someone with the hands in the
dough.
SYNONYM (1): **coger en el acto** *exp.*
• (lit); to catch in the act.
SYNONYM (2): **cachar con las
manos en la masa** *exp.* • (lit); to
seize with the hands in the
dough.

colmar a uno de *exp.* to shower
someone with • (lit); to fill
someone to the brim with.

colmo *m.* • (lit); height, culmination
• *¡Es el colmo!;* That's the limit!
(That's the last straw, etc.)

comer como un desfondado *exp.* to
eat like a pig • (lit); to eat as if
one's bottom fell off.
NOTE: The noun *desfondado* comes
from the verb *desfondar* meaning
"to go through or break the
bottom of."

como (un) pez fuera del agua *exp.*
to feel out of place, to feel like a
fish out of water • (lit); like a fish
out of water.
SYNONYM (1): **estar como perro
en barrio ajeno** *exp.* • (lit); to be

like a dog in a strange
neighborhood.
SYNONYM (2): estar como gallina
en corral ajeno *exp.* • (lit); to be
like a chicken in a strange pen.

como Pedro por su casa *exp.* as if he
owned the place • (lit); like Peter
in his house.

con el corazón en la mano *exp.* in
all frankness • (lit); with the
heart in the hand.

con los brazos abiertos *exp.* • (lit);
with open arms.
ALSO: **estar hecho un brazo de
mar** *exp.* to be dressed to kill •
(lit); to be made an arm to the
sea.

conocer *v.* to meet • (lit); to know.
NOTE: This usage of *conocer* is
extremely popular throughout
the Spanish-speaking
communities.

conocer como la palma de la mano
exp. to know backwards and
forwards • (lit); to know like the
palm of the hand.
SYNONYM (1): **saber de memoria**
exp. • (lit); to know by memory,
to know by heart (refers only to
things, not to people).
SYNONYM (2): **saber al dedillo**
exp. • (lit); to know like a finger
• NOTE: This expression applies
only to things, not to people.

conocerle el juego *exp.* to be on to
someone • (lit); to know
someone's game.

consultarlo con la almohada *exp.* to sleep on it • (lit); to consult it with the pillow.

convidar a *v.* to treat (someone) to (something) • (lit); to invite to • *Me convidó a una copa de Kahlúa;* He/She treated me to a glass of Kahlúa.

correr *v.* **1.** to drive fast, to speed • **2.** to hurry • *¡Corre! ¡Corre!* Hurry up! **3.** to fly (said of time) • *¡Cómo corre el tiempo!* How time flies! • (lit); to run.
SYNONYM: **fletado(a)** *adj.* (Venezuela, Colombia) quickly • NOTE: This comes from the verb *fletar,* meaning "to load freight."

corriente *adj.* ordinary, run-of-the-mill • (lit); (of the) current or flow.
SYNONYM: **ser del montón** *exp.* • (lit); to be of the heap or pile.

cortarle el hilo a alguien *exp.* to interrupt someone • (lit); to cut the thread of someone.
SYNONYM: **cortarle el hilo/la hebra a alguien** *exp.* • (lit); to cut the thread/filament of someone.
ALSO: **perder el hilo/la hebra de** *exp.* to lose the thread/filament of (a conversation, etc.)

costar un ojo de la cara *exp.* to cost an arm and a leg • (lit); to cost an eye from the face.
SYNONYM: **costar un huevo** *exp.* (Venezuela, Colombia, Bolivia, Ecuador, Peru) to cost an arm and a leg • (lit); to cost an egg • NOTE: In these countries, the masculine noun *huevo* is commonly used to mean "testicle."

creerse el/la muy muy *exp.* (Mexico) to be conceited, to think highly of oneself • (lit); to believe oneself the very very.
SYNONYM: **creerse la mamá de los pollitos** *exp.* • (lit); to think oneself the mother of the chickens.

cría cuervos y te sacarán los ojos *exp.* that's the thanks you get, to bite the hand that feeds you • (lit); raise crows and they will take out your eyes.

crujirle las tripas *exp.* to be hungry (lit); to have one's intestines growl.
SYNONYM (1): **estar muriendo de hambre** *exp.* • (lit); to be dying of hunger.
SYNONYM (2): **comerse los puños** *exp.* to be famished • (lit); to eat one's fists.

cuatro gatos *exp.* hardly a soul, hardly anybody • (lit); four cats.
ANTONYM: **más de cuatro** *exp.* many people.

cuento chino *exp.* cock-and-bull story • (lit); a Chinese story.

-CH-

chamaco(a) *n.* (Mexico) little boy/girl.
SYNONYM (1): **chaval(la)** *n.* (Spain) young man/woman, adolescent • ALSO: **chavalería** *f.*

kids.
SYNONYM (2): **pibe** *n.* (Argentina and Uruguay).
SYNONYM (3): **patojo(a)** *n.* (Guatemala).
SYNONYM (4): **nene** *n.* (Argentina, Uruguay, Spain).
SYNONYM (5): **guambito** *n.* (Colombia).
SYNONYM (6): **cipote** *m.* (El Salvador).
SYNONYM (7): **pelado** *m.* (Colombia).
SYNONYM (8): **cabro** *m.* (Chile).
SYNONYM (9): **guagua** *f.* (Peru, Chile, Ecuador) baby • NOTE: This is an onomatopoeia since *guagua* is the type of sound a baby makes when crying. Although *guagua* is always feminine, it may equally be used to refer to a male baby. It is important to note than in Cuba and the Canary Islands, *guagua* means "municipal bus."

chévere *adj.* (Cuba, Puerto Rico, Dominican Republic) terrific, neat.

chico(a) *n.* (Cuba, Puerto Rico, Dominican Republic) pal, chum, kid • (lit); boy/girl • *¡Hola, chico!* Hi, kid!
SYNONYM: **hermano(a)** *n.* • (lit); brother/sister • *¡Mi hermano!* Hey pal!

chismear *v.* to gossip
NOTE: **chisme** *m.* a juicy piece of gossip • *¡Cuéntame los chismes!;* Give me the dirt!
SYNONYM: **chispazo** *m.* • (lit); spark.

ALSO: **chismorrear** *v.* to gossip, to blab (a variant of *chismear*).

-D-

dar a luz a *exp.* **1.** to give birth to • **2.** to publish • (lit); to give light to.
ALSO: **en plena luz** *exp.* in broad daylight • (lit); in full light.

dar calabazas a uno *exp.* **1.** to fail someone • **2.** to jilt someone • (lit); to give someone pumpkins.
NOTE (1): **recibir calabazas** *exp.* **1.** to fail (a test) • **2.** to get jilted • (lit); to receive pumpkins.
NOTE (2): Interestingly enough, an amusing variation of the expression *dar calabazas* has been created in which the feminine noun *calabaza* meaning "pumpkin" has been transformed into the slang verb *calabacear* meaning "to fail (someone) or to jilt" or literally, "to pumpkin (someone)."

dar de baja *exp.* to drop (from a team, list, etc.), dismiss, discharge, fire • (lit); to give from under.
ALSO: **por lo bajo** *exp.* on the sly.

dar en el clavo *exp.* to hit the nail on the head, to put one's finger on it • (lit); to hit on the nail.
ALSO: **ser capaz de clavar un clavo con la cabeza** *exp.* to be pigheaded, stubborn • (lit); to be capable of hammering a nail with the head.
SYNONYM: **dar en el hito** *exp.* •

(lit); to hit on the stone.
NOTE: **dar en** *exp.* to hit on • (lit);
to give on.

dar gato por liebre *exp.* to cheat,
deceive, put something over on
someone • (lit); to give cat for
hare.
SYNONYM (1): **hacerle guaje a uno**
exp. (Mexico) • (lit); to make a
fool of someone.
SYNONYM (2): **pasársela a uno**
exp. (Chile) • (lit); to go too far
with someone.

dar lo mismo *exp.* to make no
difference • (lit); to give the
same.

dar una vuelta *exp.* to take a walk, a
stroll • (lit); to give a turn.
SYNONYM (1): **dar un paseo** *exp.* •
(lit); to give a passage.
SYNONYM (2): **pasear a pie** *exp.* •
(lit); to walk by foot.

darle coba a uno *exp.* to soft-soap
someone, to suck up to someone
• (lit); to give flattery to someone.

darle mala espina *exp.* to worry
one, to make one feel uneasy •
(lit); to give one a bad thorn.

darse lija *exp.* (Cuba, Puerto Rico,
Dominican Republic) to put on
airs, to act pretentious • (lit); to
give oneself sandpaper.
SYNONYM (1): **darse tono** *exp.* •
(lit); to give oneself tone (or "to
give off a pretentious tone").
SYNONYM (2): **subirse de tono** *exp.*
• (lit); to get on a tone.
SYNONYM (3): **darse mucho taco**
exp. (Mexico) • (lit); to give
oneself much heel.

SYNONYM (4): **botarse el pucho**
exp. (Chile) • (lit); to bounce a
cigarette.
SYNONYM (5): **darse corte/darse
paquete** *exp.* (Ecuador) • (lit); to
give oneself length/to give
oneself package.

de buenas a primeras *exp.*
suddenly (and unexpectedly),
right off the bat, from the very
start • (lit); from the good ones
to the first ones.
ALSO: **bueno(a)** *adj.* nasty, bad •
(lit); good • *Tiene una buena gripe;*
He/She has a nasty flu. •NOTE:
This could be compared to the
American expression "to have a
real good cold" where "real
good" actually refers to
something that is nasty or
disagreeable.
SYNONYM: **luego luego** *adv.* right
away • (lit); later later • NOTE:
Although its literal translation is
indeed "later later," when *luego*
is repeated twice, it means,
oddly enough, "right away,
immediately."

de cabo a rabo *exp.* from beginning
to end • (lit); from end to tail.
SYNONYM (1): **de cabo a cabo** *exp.*
• (lit); from end to end.
SYNONYM (2): **de punta a punta**
exp. • (lit); from point to point.
ALSO: **no dejar cabo suelto** *exp.*
not to leave any loose ends •
(lit); not to leave loose end.

de cuando en cuando *exp.*
sometimes, occasionally • (lit);
from when to when.
SYNONYM: **de vez en cuando** *exp.*
• (lit); from time to when.

de hecho *exp.* in fact • (lit); of fact.

de primera *exp.* first-rate, the best • (lit); of first.

de tal palo, tal astilla *exp.* like father, like son • (lit); from such a stick, such a splinter.
SYNONYM (1): **de casta le viene al galgo ser rabilargo** *exp.* like father, like son • (lit); from the breed the greyhound gets to be long-tailed.
SYNONYM (2): **cual el cuervo, tal su huevo** *exp.* • (lit); like the raven, like the egg.
SYNONYM (3): **de tal jarro, tal tepalcate** *exp.* (Mexico).

de todas maneras *exp.* at any rate, in any case, anyway • (lit); in all manners.
SYNONYM: **de todos modos** *exp.* • (lit); in all modes.

de todos modos *exp.* anyway, at any rate • (lit); in all modes.

de un modo u otro *exp.* one way or another, somehow • (lit); of one manner or another.

de una vez y para siempre *exp.* once and for all • (lit); for one time and for always.
SYNONYM: **de una vez** *exp.* • (lit); for one time.

de veras *exp.* really, honestly, is that so • (lit); from truth.

¿de qué se trata? *exp.* what's it about? what does it deal with? • (lit); of what does it discuss/deal?

decir amén a todo *exp.* to be a yes-man • (lit); to say Amen to everything.

defenderse *v.* to get along, not to do badly, to be able to handle (a particular task) • (lit); to defend oneself.

dejar alguien plantado(a) *exp.* **1.** to stand someone up • (lit); to leave someone planted • **2.** to leave someone in the lurch, to walk out on someone.
ALSO: **bien plantado(a)** *adj.* handsome, well-turned out • (lit); well-planted.
SYNONYM (1): **dejar en las astas del toro** *exp.* • (lit); to leave in the spears of the bull.
SYNONYM (2): **dejar a uno embarcado** *exp.* (Mexico) • (lit); to leave someone embarked.

del dicho al hecho hay mucho/gran trecho *exp.* easier said than done • (lit); from the saying to the doing, there is much/great distance.

descomponerse *v.* to break down (said of a car) • (lit); to decompose.
SYNONYM (1): **accidentado(a)** *adj.* **1.** (Venezuela) broken-down (applied to a car) • **2.** bumpy (applied to a road) • (lit); uneven (applied to roads).
SYNONYM (2): **estar descompuesto(a)** *adj.* (Mexico) • (lit); to be decomposed • *un motor descompuesto;* a broken-down motor.
SYNONYM (3): **tener una avería** *exp.* (Spain) • (lit); to have

injuries • *El coche tiene una avería;* There is a problem with the car.
SYNONYM (4): **tener un pane/una pana** *exp.* (Peru, Ecuador).
SYNONYM (5): **una descompostura** *v.* (Mexico) This comes from the verb *descomponer* meaning "to break down." • NOTE: **composturas** *f.pl.* (Mexico) car repairs.
SYNONYM (6): **roto(a)** *adj.* (Cuba).

desde luego *exp.* certainly, of course • (lit); since then.
SYNONYM: **por supuesto** *exp.* of course, certainly • (lit); for supposed.

deshacerse de *v.* to get rid of • (lit); to undo oneself of.
ALSO: **deshacerse por (uno)** *exp.* to go out of one's way for someone, to outdo oneself for •
SEE: *Lesson Two – Vocabulary*, p. 17.

deshacerse por *exp.* to bust one's buns in order to do something, to bend over backwards • (lit); to undo oneself for.

dichosos los ojos *exp.* how nice to see you • (lit); fortunate the eyes.
ALSO: **costar/valer un ojo de la cara** *exp.* to cost an arm and a leg • (lit); to cost/to be worth an eye of the face.

Dios los cría y ellos se juntan *exp.* birds of a feather flock together • (lit); God raises them and they get together.

¡Dios me libre! *interj.* God forbid! • (lit); God free me!

SYNONYM: **¡Vaya por Dios!** *exp.* • Good God! (lit); Go by God!

dulzura *f.* sweetheart • (lit); sweetness.
NOTE: Other terms of endearment include: *mi alma, mi cielo, mi cariño, amor mío, mi amor, mi pichón, mi corazón, etc.*

-E-

echar a alguien a la calle *exp.* to fire someone, to can someone • (lit); to throw someone to the street.
SYNONYM: **correr** *v.* • (lit); to run • *Lo corrieron;* He was fired. •
NOTE: In this example, the verb *correr* could be loosely translated as "to run someone off."

echar espumarajos por la boca *exp.* to be furious, to foam at the mouth with rage • (lit); to throw foam from the mouth.
SYNONYM: **enchilarse** *v.* (Mexico) • (lit); to get red in the face from eating chilies.

echar flores a alguien *exp.* to flatter someone, to soft-soap someone, to butter someone up • (lit); to throw flowers at someone.
SYNONYM (1): **pasar la mano por el lomo** *exp.* • (lit); to pass the hand by the back.
SYNONYM (2): **darle la suave a uno** *exp.* • (lit); to give the soft to someone.
SYNONYM (3): **ser barbero** *exp.* (Mexico) • (lit); to be a barber.
SYNONYM (4): **pasarle la mano a**

alguien *exp.* • (lit); to pass one's hand to someone.

echar las tripas *exp.* to throw up one's guts • (lit); to throw guts/tripes.
SYNONYM: **arrojar** *v.* to throw up • (lit); to throw.

echar un sueño *exp.* to take a nap • (lit); to throw a sleep.
SYNONYM (1): **tomar una siestesita** *exp.* to take a little nap • (lit); to throw/sleep a little siesta.
SYNONYM (2): **echar/dormir una siestesita** *exp.* (Cuba, Puerto Rico, Dominican Republic) • (lit); to throw/sleep a little nap.
SYNONYM (3): **tomar una pestañita** *exp.* (Mexico) to get some shut-eye • (lit); to take a little eyelash.
SYNONYM (4): **dormir la siesta** *exp.* • (lit); to sleep the nap.
SYNONYM (5): **echar un pestañazo** *exp.* (Cuba, Puerto Rico, Dominican Republic).
ALSO (1): **dormir a pierna suelta** *exp.* to sleep soundly • (lit); to sleep with loose legs.
ALSO (2): **pasar la noche en claro/en blanco** *exp.* not to sleep a wink • (lit); to spend the night in brightness/in blank.
ALSO (3): **dormir como un lirón** *exp.* to sleep like a log • (lit); to sleep like a dormouse.
ALSO (4): **dormir como un tronco** *exp.* to sleep like a log • (lit); to sleep like a trunk (of a tree).
ALSO (5): **estar en los brazos de Morfeo** *exp.* to sleep soundly • (lit); to be in the arms of Morpheus (the son of sleep and the god of dreams, according to Ovid).

echar/tirar la casa por la ventana *exp.* to go overboard • (lit); to throw the house out the window.
ALSO: **sentirse como en casa** *exp.* to feel right at home • (lit); to feel like in home.

echarle el ojo a algo/alguien *exp.* to make eyes at something/someone • (lit); to throw the eye at something/someone.
SYNONYM (1): **hacerle ojos a alguien** *exp.* • (lit); to make eyes at someone.
SYNONYM (2): **comerse con los ojos** *exp.* • (lit); to eat someone up with one's eyes.

echarle una mano a uno *exp.* to lend someone a hand • (lit); to throw someone a hand.
SYNONYM: **dar una mano** *exp.* • (lit); to give a hand.

echarse atrás *exp.* to back out • (lit); to throw oneself backwards
ALSO: **volverse/echarse para atrás** *exp.* to go back on one's word • (lit); to turn/to throw oneself backwards.

echarse flores *f.pl.* to toot one's own horn, to flatter oneself • (lit); to throw oneself flowers.
ALSO: **echarle flores a alguien** *exp.* to flatter someone, to sweet-talk someone • (lit); to throw flowers at someone.

echarse un trago *exp.* to have oneself a drink • (lit); to throw a swallow.

NOTE (1): The verb *tragar*, which literally means "to swallow," is commonly used to mean "to eat voraciously." It is interesting to note that as a noun, *trago* means "a drink." However, when used as a verb, *tragar* takes on the meaning of "to eat": *¿Quieres echar un trago?*; Would you care for a drink? • *¿Qué quieres tragar?*; What would you like to eat?

SYNONYM (1): **empinar el codo** *exp.* • (lit); to raise the elbow.

SYNONYM (2): **echarse un fogonazo** *exp.* (Mexico) • (lit); to throw oneself a flash.

SYNONYM (3): **empinar el cacho** *exp.* (Chile) • (lit); to raise the piece.

SYNONYM (4): **pegarse un palo** *exp.* (Cuba, Puerto Rico, Dominican Republic, Colombia) • (lit); to stick oneself a gulp.

SYNONYM (5): **darse un palo** *exp.* (Cuba) • (lit); to give oneself a gulp.

ALSO: **duro de tragar** *exp.* hard to believe • (lit); hard to swallow.

el hábito no hace al monje *exp.* you can't judge a book by it's cover • (lit); the habit doesn't make the monk.

SYNONYM: **caras vemos, corazones no sabemos** *exp.* • (lit); faces we see, hearts we don't know.

el que la hace la paga *exp.* what goes around comes around, one must pay the consequences • (lit); he who does it pays for it.

emborracharse a muerte *adv.* to get dead drunk • (lit); to get drunk to death.

SYNONYM: **coger una borrachera** *exp.* • (lit); to catch a drunken state

ANTONYM: **dormir la mona** *exp.* to sleep it off • (lit); to sleep the monkey.

NOTE: **estar crudo** *exp.* to have a hangover • (lit); to be raw • *la cruda*; hangover.

emperifollarse *v.* to get all dressed up, to dress to kill • (lit); to decorate or adorn oneself.

SYNONYM (1): **acicalarse** *v.* • (lit); to polish oneself.

SYNONYM (2): **de etiqueta** *exp.* (used only for a man) formal, full dress • (lit); of etiquette, of ceremony • ALSO: **vestirse de etiqueta** *exp.* (used only for a man) to get all dressed up • (lit); to clothe oneself of etiquette.

empinar el codo *exp.* to drink, to tipple • (lit); to raise the elbow.

SYNONYM: **chupar la botella** *exp.* • (lit); to suck the bottle.

en cambio *exp.* but, on the other hand • (lit); in exchange.

en cueros *exp.* naked, in one's birthday suit • (lit); in (one's own) hide.

SYNONYM (1): **en traje de Adán** *exp.* • (lit); in the suit of Adam.

SYNONYM (2): **en pelota** *exp.* • (lit); in balls.

SYNONYM (3): **pila** *f.* (Ecuador, Peru, Bolivia) • (lit); heap, pile.

ALSO (1): **encuerado(a)** *adj.* • (lit); skinned.

ALSO (2): **en cueros vivos** *exp.* stark-naked • (lit); in (one's own) living hide.

en el acto *exp.* **1.** immediately, on the spot • **2.** in the act (of doing something) • (lit); in the act. SYNONYM: **acto continuo/seguido** *exp.* • (lit); continuous/consecutive act.

en fin *exp.* in short • (lit); in the end • *En fin, es estúpido;* In short, he's stupid.

en las barbas *exp.* in one's face • (lit); in one's beards. ALSO: **reírse en las barbas de uno** *exp.* to laugh in one's face • (lit); to laugh in one's beards.

en menos que canta un gallo *exp.* in a flash, in a jiffy, in two shakes of a lamb's tail • (lit); in less (time) than a rooster sings (crows). ALSO: **entre gallos y media noche** *exp.* at an unearthly hour • (lit); between roosters and midnight.

en pleno(a) *adj.* in the middle of • (lit); in full • *¡Los niños estaban jugando en plena calle!;* The children were playing in the middle of the street! • *en pleno día;* in broad daylight.

en punto *exp.* on the dot, sharp • (lit); on the point.

en resumidas cuentas *exp.* in brief, in short, getting to the bottom line • (lit); in summarized calculations. SYNONYM (1): **en resumen** *exp.* •

(lit); in summary. SYNONYM (2): **en resolución** *exp.* • (lit); in resolution. SYNONYM (3): **al fin y al cabo** *exp.* • (lit); to the end and the end.

encima de todo *exp.* on top of everything.

engañar a uno *exp.* to fool someone, to deceive someone, to cheat on someone • (lit); to deceive someone.

enredarse con alguien *exp.* to have an affair with someone • (lit); to become entangled with someone. SYNONYM (1): **aventura amorosa** *exp.* • (lit); amorous adventure. SYNONYM (2): **estar metido(a) con alguien** *exp.* • (lit); to be placed with someone.

entenderse bien con alguien *exp.* to get along with someone • (lit); to understand each other well. SYNONYM: **llevarse bien con alguien** • (lit); to carry oneself well with someone.

enterarse *v.* to find out, to get to know • (lit); to inform oneself.

entrar por un oído y salir por el otro *exp.* to go in one ear and out the other. ALSO: **ser todos oídos** *exp.* to be all ears.

entre paréntesis *exp.* by the way, incidentally • (lit); in parentheses.

eso lo sabe hasta el gato *exp.* everyone knows that, that's common knowledge • (lit); even the cat knows that.

estar (uno) hasta la coronilla de *exp.* to be fed up with, to have had it up to here with • (lit); to be up to the crown of one's head with.
SYNONYM: **estar hasta la punta del pelo (de)** *exp.* • (lit); to be up to the ends of the hair with •
ALSO: **estar hasta los pelos (de)** *exp.* • (lit); to be up to the hairs with.

estar a dos dedos de *exp.* to be on the verge of • (lit); to be two fingers from.
SYNONYM: **dedo** *m.* a little bit • (lit); finger • *Beber un dedo de vino;* To drink a drop of wine.

estar a la mira *exp.* to be on the lookout • (lit); to be on the look.
NOTE: This comes from the verb *mirar* meaning "to look."
SYNONYM: **estar truchas** *exp.* • (lit); to be trouts (because of their large wide open eyes).

estar a punto de *exp.* • (lit); to be on the point of • NOTE: This expression is always followed by a verb, i.e. *Estuve al punto de llorar;* I was on the verge of crying.
SYNONYM (1): **estar al borde de** *exp.* to be on the verge of, to be on the brink of • (lit); to be on the edge of • NOTE: This expression is always followed by a noun, i.e. *Estuve al borde del llanto;* I was on the brink of tears.
SYNONYM (2): **estar a dos dedos de** *exp.* • (lit); to be two fingers

(away) from • NOTE: This expression is always followed by a verb, i.e. *Estuve a dos dedos de gritar;* I was on the verge of screaming.

estar agotado(a) *adj.* to be exhausted, be completely tired out • (lit); to be emptied or drained.
SYNONYM (1): **estar/sentirse como un trapo viejo** *exp.* • (lit); to feel like an old rag.
SYNONYM (2): **estar rendido** *exp.* • (lit); to be rendered (of all one's energy).
SYNONYM (3): **estar reventado** *exp.* • (lit); to be burst (like a balloon whose air has suddenly been let out).

estar al borde del llanto *exp.* to be on the verge of tears • (lit); to be on the edge of weeping.

estar bien conservado(a) *exp.* • (lit); to be well-preserved.
ANTONYM: **estar con piel de pasa** *exp.* to look old • (lit); to be with raisin skin.

estar bien envuelto(a) en carne *exp.* to be plump, to be fat • (lit); to be well-wrapped in flesh.
ALSO: **en carne viva** *exp.* raw, without skin • (lit); in live flesh.

estar bravo(a) *exp.* **1.** to be ill-tempered • **2.** (Chile) hot, highly seasoned • **3.** (Cuba) angry • (lit); fierce, ferocious.
SYNONYM (1): **levantarse del pie izquierdo** *exp.* to get up on the wrong side of the bed • (lit); to get up on the left foot.

estar como un pez en el agua *exp.* to be in one's element, to feel right at home • (lit); to be like a fish in the water.
ALSO: **pez gordo** *m.* big shot, bigwig • (lit); fat fish.
NOTE: **pez** is a live fish; **pescado** is a fish that has been prepared as food.

estar cosido(a) a las faldas de *exp.* to be tied to the apron strings of • (lit); to be sewn to the skirts of.
ALSO: **andar siempre entre faldas** *exp.* to be always with the girls • (lit); to go always with skirts.

estar crudo(a) *exp.* (Mexico) to have a hangover • (lit); to be raw •
ALSO: **tener una cruda** *exp.*
SYNONYM (1): **tener resaca** *exp.* (Eastern Argentina, Uruguay) • (lit); to have undertow.
SYNONYM (2): **tener un ratón** *exp.* (Venezuela, Colombia, Ecuador, Peru, Bolivia) • (lit); to have a mouse • ALSO: **estar enratonado(a)** *exp.* • (lit); to be "moused."
SYNONYM (3): **tener la mona** *exp.* (Chile) • (lit); to have the monkey.
SYNONYM (4): **estar de goma** *exp.* (Central America) • (lit); to be of rubber.

estar de gala *exp.* to be all dressed up, to be in formal attire, to be dressed to kill • (lit); to be in full regalia.

estar de humor de perros *exp.* to be in a lousy mood • (lit); to be in the mood of dogs.

SYNONYM: **tener malas pulgas**.
NOTE: The expression *de perros* meaning "lousy" can be used to modify other nouns as well. A variation of *de perros* is *perro(a)*. For example, *Pasé una noche perra;* I had a hell of a night.
ALSO (1): **a otro perro con ese hueso** *exp.* don't give me that baloney, get out of here, come off it • (lit); to another dog with that bone.
ALSO (2): **perro viejo** *exp.* cunning and experienced individual, sly old dog • (lit); old dog.

estar de moda *exp.* to be fashionable, to be chic • (lit); to be of fashion.
SYNONYM: **de buen tono** *exp.* • (lit); of good tone.

estar de parranda *exp.* to be out partying.
SYNONYM (1): **andar de parranda** *exp.* to go out partying.
SYNONYM (2): **parrandear** *v.* to go out partying.
SYNONYM (3): **irse de juerga** *exp.* to paint the town red • (lit); to go on a binge.
SYNONYM (4): **irse de tuna** *exp.* (Colombia) to go on a spree, to paint the town red • (lit); to go (running around) for female students.
SYNONYM (5): **irse de farras** *exp.* (Eastern Argentina, Uruguay) to party it up • (lit); to go for lavarets (a type of fish).
SYNONYM (6): **irse de jarana** *exp.* (Venezuela) to go partying, to go on a binge • (lit); to go make a rumpus, a lot of noise.

SYNONYM (7): **irse de rumba** *exp.* (Cuba, Puerto Rico, Dominican Republic) to go partying • (lit); to go for a rumba.
NOTE (1): **parrandero(a)** *n.* party animal.
NOTE (2): **parrandeo** *m.* party.
NOTE (3): **pachanga** *f.* party.

estar echando chispas *exp.* to be hopping mad, to spit fire • (lit); to throw sparks.
ALSO (1): **chispa** *f.* drunkenness •
NOTE: **chisparse** *v.* to get drunk • (lit); to "spark up."
ALSO (2): **tener chispa** *exp.* to be witty • (lit); to have spark.

estar en las mismas *exp.* to be in the same boat • (lit); to be in the same (ones).

estar en las nubes *exp.* to be daydreaming • (lit); to be in the clouds.
SYNONYM: **estar soñando** *adj.* • (lit); to be in a dreamlike state •
NOTE: This comes from the verb *soñar* meaning "to dream."

estar en un apuro *m.* to be in a difficult situation, in a jam • (lit); to be in a difficulty.
ANTONYM: **sacar del apuro** *exp.* to get out of a jam • (lit); to get out of a difficulty.

estar fichado(a) *adj.* to be on someone's blacklist • (lit); to be filed on a card, to be indexed.
ALSO: **fichar** *v.* to figure someone out, to have someone's number • *Le tengo bien fichado;* I've got him figured out.

estar harto(a) de alguien *exp.* • to be fed up with someone, to be sick and tired of someone (lit); to be full of someone.
SYNONYM (1): **alucinar a alguien** *exp.* • (lit); to hallucinate someone •
NOTE: This could be loosely translated as "to see someone in one's worst dreams."
SYNONYM (2): **tener a uno entre cejas** *exp.* • (lit); to have someone between eyebrows.
SYNONYM (3): **tener a uno entre ceja y ceja** *exp.* not to be able to stand someone • (lit); to have someone between eyebrow and eyebrow • ALSO: **estar hasta las cejas de** *exp.* to be fed up with, to have had it up to here • (lit); to be up to the eyebrows with • *Estoy hasta las cejas de mi trabajo;* I've had it with my work.
SYNONYM: **tenerle a uno hasta en la sopa** *exp.* to have one satiated in soup.

estar hecho(a) una sopa *exp.* to be drenched • (lit); to be made into a soup.
ALSO: **comer de la sopa boba** *exp.* to live off others.

estar loco(a) de remate *exp.* to be stark-raving mad, to be nuts • (lit); to be crazy to the end.
ALSO (1): **como remate** *exp.* to top it off • *Y como remate perdí mis libros;* And to top it off, I lost my books.
ALSO (2): **para remate** *exp.* to crown it all, on top of all that • (lit); to end.
ALSO (3): **por remate** *exp.* finally,

in the end, as a finishing touch •
(lit); by end.

estar muriéndose de ganas por *exp.*
to be dying to do something •
(lit); to be dying with desire to.
SYNONYM (1): **estar frito por
hacer algo** *exp.* • (lit); to be fried
to do something (English
equivalent: "to be burning to do
something").
SYNONYM (2): **comerse de envidia
por hacer algo** *exp.* • (lit); to eat
oneself up with desire to do
something.
SYNONYM (3): **estar en plan de**
exp. • (lit); to be in the scheme of
[or] to have the mind set to.

estar podrido(a) en dinero *exp.* to
be filthy-rich, stinking-rich •
(lit); to be rotten in money.
SYNONYM (1): **tener más lana que
un borrego** *exp.* • (lit); to have
more wool than a lamb • NOTE:
This is actually a humorous play
on words since the feminine
noun *lana*, which literally
translates as "wool," is also used
to connote "money, loot,
dough." An equivalent
expression might be, "He
hasamen more dough than a
baker."
SYNONYM (2): **tener el riñón bien
cubierto** *exp.* • (lit); to have a
well-covered kidney.
SYNONYM (3): **estar bien
parado(a)** *exp.* • (lit); to be
standing up well.
SYNONYM (4): **tener la canasta
baja y el riñón bien cubierto**
exp. (Mexico) • (lit); to have the

basket low and the kidney
well-covered.

estar por las nubes *exp.* to be
sky-high • (lit); to be around the
clouds.
ALSO: **ponerse por las nubes** *exp.*
to make (prices) soar sky-high •
*Los precios se pusieron por las
nubes;* The prices were sky-high.

**estar siempre con la misma
cantaleta** *exp.* to harp on the
same string, to have a one-track
mind • (lit); to be always with
the same serenade.
SYNONYM: **estar siempre con la
misma letanía** *exp.* • (lit); to be
always with the same litany.

estar sin un quinto *exp.* to be flat
broke • (lit); to be without a fifth.
SYNONYM (1): **brotar el dinero
por las orejas (a alguien)** *exp.* •
(lit); to sprout money through
the ears (of someone).
SYNONYM (2): **estar arrancado(a)**
exp. • (lit); to be uprooted.
SYNONYM (3): **estar pato** *exp.*
(Chile) • (lit); to be duck.
SYNONYM (4): **estar pelado(a)** *exp.*
• (lit); to be peeled.
SYNONYM (5): **no tener un real**
exp. (Spain) • (lit); not to have a
real (a Spanish coin worth
one-fourth of a peseta).
SYNONYM (6): **no tener un duro**
exp. (Spain) • (lit); not to have a
duro (a Spanish dollar).

estar sobre/en ascuas *exp.* to be on
pins and needles • (lit); to be on
embers (or glowing embers).
NOTE: **ascua** *f.* • (lit); live coal.

estar tan claro(a) como el agua *exp.*
to be crystal clear (i.e. a concept,
etc.) • (lit); to be as clear as the
water.

estar/hallarse en el pellejo de otro
exp. to be in somebody else's
shoes • (lit); to be in the skin of
another.

-F-

faltar un tornillo *exp.* to be crazy, to
have a screw loose • (lit); to miss
a screw • *Le falta un tornillo;*
He's/She's missing a screw.
SYNONYM (1): **tener flojos los
tornillos** *exp.* • (lit); to have
loose screws.
SYNONYM (2): **estar chiflado(a)**
exp. • (lit); to be crazy, cracked.
SYNONYM (3): **tener los alambres
pelados** *exp.* (Chile) • (lit); to
have smooth bells.

-G-

ganarse la vida *exp.* to earn one's
living • (lit); to earn one's life.

gastar saliva en balde *exp.* to waste
one's breath (while explaining
something to someone) • **1.
gastar saliva** *exp.* to waste one's
breath • (lit); to waste one's
saliva • **2. en balde** *exp.* for
nothing, in vain • (lit); in a pail,
bucket.
ALSO: **de balde** *exp.* free of charge.

gritar como un descosido *exp.* to
scream one's lungs out, to
scream out of control • (lit); to
scream like something
unstitched.
NOTE: This expression comes
from the verb *descoser* meaning
"to unstitch." Therefore, this
expression could be loosely
translated as "to come apart at
the seams."
ALSO: **beber/comer/correr como
un descosido** *exp.* to
drink/eat/run like crazy.

guardar cama *exp.* to stay in bed, to
be confined to bed • (lit); to keep
bed.

gústete o no *exp.* whether you like
it or not • (lit); like it or not.

-H-

hablar a mil por hora *exp.* to talk
non-stop • (lit); to talk a
thousand (miles) per hour.

hablar como loco(a) *exp.* to speak
nonstop • (lit); to speak like
crazy, like mad.
NOTE: **como loco(a)** *exp.* like
crazy, like mad • *correr como loco;*
to run like mad.
ALSO: **tener una suerte loca** *exp.*
to have unbelievable luck • (lit);
to have (a) crazy luck.
SYNONYM (1): **hablar como una
cotorra** *exp.* • (lit); to talk like a
magpie.
SYNONYM (2): **no parar la boca**
exp. (Mexico) • (lit); not to stop
(flapping) one's mouth.

SYNONYM (3): **hablar hasta por los codos** *exp.* • (lit); to talk even with the elbows.

SYNONYM (4): **ser lengua larga** *exp.* to gossip • (lit); to be long-tongued.

hacer acto de presencia *exp.* to put in an appearance • (lit); to make an act of presence.

hacer añicos *exp.* 1. (of objects) to smash to smithereens • 2. (of paper) to rip to shreds • (lit); to make (into) fragments or bits.
ALSO: **estar hecho añicos** *exp.* to be worn out, exhausted • (lit); to be made into fragments or bits.

hacer buenas migas *exp.* to get along with someone, to hit it off well • (lit); to make good crumbs (together).
ANTONYM: **hacer malas migas** *exp.* not to get along with someone, not to hit it off well • (lit); to make bad crumbs (together).

hacer el equipaje *exp.* to pack one's bags • (lit); to do one's baggage.

hacer furor *exp.* to be a big event, to make a big splash • (lit); to make fury.
SYNONYM: **tener un éxito padre** *exp.* to be a huge success • (lit); to have a huge success • SEE: **padre**.

hacer la barba a alguien *exp.* to butter (someone) up, to kiss up to (someone) • (lit); to shave someone's beard.
ALSO: **reírse en las barbas de uno** *exp.* to laugh in someone's face • (lit); to laugh in someone's beard.

hacer la pinta *exp.* to cut class • (lit); to make the spot.
NOTE: This is a humorous expression which conjures up an image of someone leaving behind nothing more than a spot or mark as proof that he/she was once there.
SYNONYM: **fumarse una clase** *exp.* to cut a class • (lit); to smoke a class.

hacer las paces *exp.* to make up after a quarrel • (lit); to make peace.
ANTONYM: **romper con** *exp.* to have a falling out • (lit); to break with.

hacer mal/buen papel *exp.* to make a bad/good impression • *Hiciste buen papel anoche;* You made a good impression last night • (lit); to do a bad/good (theatrical) role.

hacer puente *exp.* to take a long weekend • (lit); to make a bridge (between Sunday and Monday).
ALSO: **puente** *m.* long weekend • (lit); bridge.

hacerse ilusiones *exp.* to fool oneself, to delude oneself • (lit); to make oneself illusions.

hacerse noche *exp.* to get dark, to get late in the afternoon • (lit); to make itself (to become) night.
SYNONYM: **hacerse tarde** *exp.* to become late • (lit); to make itself late.

hacérsele a uno un nudo en la garganta *exp.* to get a lump in one's throat • (lit); to have a knot form in one's throat.
ALSO: **tener buena garganta** *exp.* to have a good voice • (lit); to have (a) good throat • NOTE: This could best be compared to the expression "to have a golden throat."

hacérsele agua la boca *exp.* to make one's mouth water • (lit); to turn one's mouth into water.

¡hombre! *interj.* man alive!, come on! • (lit); man.

borrowed from English and has become a popular replacement for the standard expression for "picnic," *día de campo*.

ir de vacaciones *exp.* to go on vacation • (lit); to go of vacations.
ALSO: **estar de vacaciones** *exp.* to be on vacation • (lit); to be of vacations.
NOTE: The feminine noun *vacaciones* is always in the plural form.
SYNONYM: **estar de viaje** *exp.* • (lit); to be of trip.

-I-

ir a medias *exp.* to go to halves, fifty-fifty • (lit); to go to halves.
SYNONYM (1): **ir a la mitad** *exp.* • (lit); to go to the half.
SYNONYM (2): **ir mitad mitad** *exp.* • (lit); to go half-half.

ir al asunto *exp.* to get down to the facts • (lit); to go to the subject.

ir al cine *exp.* to go to the movies • (lit); to go to the movie house.

ir al grano *exp.* to get to the point • (lit); to go to the seed.
NOTE: This could best be compared to the American expression, "to get to the heart of the matter."
SYNONYM: **llegar al caso** *exp.* • (lit); to arrive to the case.

ir de picnic *m.* to go on a picnic.
NOTE: This term has been

-J-

jalarse *v.* to get drunk • (lit); to pull oneself.
ALSO: **jalado(a)** *adj.* drunk, bombed, plastered.
SYNONYM (1): **pedo** *adj.* (Mexico) drunk, bombed • (lit); fart.
SYNONYM (2): **cuete** *adj.* (Mexico) drunk, bombed.
SYNONYM (3): **tomado** *adj.* (Cuba, Puerto Rico, Dominican Republic) drunk, bombed.
SYNONYM (4): **mamado** *adj.* (Eastern Argentina, Uruguay) drunk, bombed.
SYNONYM (5): **bolo** *adj.* (Central America) drunk, bombed.
SYNONYM (6): **chufifo** *adj.* (Chile) drunk, bombed.

jalarse de los pelos *exp.* (Mexico) to squabble, to fight • (lit); to pull from one's hairs.

jugarse el todo por el todo *exp.* to risk everything, to go for it • (lit); to play (or risk) everything for everything.

-L-

la cosa está que arde *exp.* things are getting hot, things are coming to a head • (lit); the thing is burning • *La cosa está que arde;* Things are coming to a head.
NOTE: **arder** *v.* • (lit); to burn.
ALSO: **arder de/en ira** *exp.* to be furious • (lit); to burn with anger.
SYNONYM (1): **estar hecho una furia** *exp.* • (lit); to become a fury.
SYNONYM (2): **estar como agua para chocolate** *exp.* • (lit); to be like water for chocolate.
SYNONYM (3): **estar hecho un chivo** *exp.* • (lit); to become a kid (young goat).

la gota que derrama el vaso *exp.* the last straw, the straw that broke the camel's back • (lit); the drop that makes the glass spill over.
SYNONYM (1): **¡No faltaba más! / ¡Lo que faltaba! / ¡Sólo faltaba eso!** *exp.* That's the last straw! • (lit); Nothing else was missing! / What was missing! / Only that was missing!
SYNONYM (2): **la última gota que hace rebasar la copa** *exp.* • (lit); the last drop that makes the glass overflow.
SYNONYM (3): **es el colmo** *exp.* • (lit); it is the height (or: that's the limit).

la niña de sus ojos *exp.* the apple of one's eye, darling, treasure • (lit); the little girl of one's eyes.
NOTE: **niña del ojo** *exp.* pupil (of the eye).
ALSO: **¡mucho ojo!** *exp.* Watch out! Be careful! • (lit); much eye • NOTE: This expression is commonly shortened simply to *¡Ojo!* Watch out!

lágrimas de cocodrilo *exp.* • (lit); crocodile tears.
ALSO (1): **beberse/tragarse las lágrimas** *exp.* to hold back one's tears • (lit); to drink/to swallow one's tears.
ALSO (2): **ser el paño de lágrimas de alguien** *exp.* to give someone a shoulder to cry on • (lit); to be someone's tear cloth.

lana *f.* money, "dough" • (lit); wool.
SYNONYM: **pasta** *f.* (Spain)

largarse *v.* to leave • (lit); to loosen, to let go, to set free.

las malas lenguas *exp.* rumor has it • (lit); the bad (or evil) tongues.
SYNONYM (1): **corre la voz que** *exp.* • (lit); the voice runs that.
SYNONYM (2): **corre la bola** *exp.* • (lit); the ball runs.

-LL-

llamar al pan pan y al vino vino *exp.* to call a spade a spade, to call it like it is • (lit); to call bread, bread and wine, wine.

llevar la batuta *exp.* to run the show • (lit); to carry the (conductor's) baton.

llevar los pantalones *exp.* to wear the pants • (lit); to wear the pants.
SYNONYM: **llevar los calzones** *exp.* • (lit); to wear the trousers.

llevarle/seguirle la corriente a uno *exp.* to humor someone • (lit); to carry/ follow the current to someone.
ALSO: **corriente** *adj.* • (lit); flow • **1.** common, ordinary • **2.** cheap • *una mujer corriente;* a cheap woman • NOTE: This comes from the verb *correr* meaning "to run." Therefore, *una corriente* could be loosely translated as "a woman who runs around with more than one man."

llevarse bien con alguien *exp.* to get along well with someone • (lit); to carry oneself well with someone.
ANTONYM: **llevarse mal con alguien** *exp.* not to get along with someone • (lit); to carry oneself badly with someone.

llevarse bien/mal con *exp.* to get/not to get along well with • (lit); to carry oneself off well/badly with.
ALSO: **hacer buenas migas** *exp.* to hit it off • (lit); to make good crumbs (together).

llevarse como perro y gato *exp.* to fight like cat and dog • (lit); to carry each other like dog and cat • NOTE: This is always used in reference to two or more people.
SEE: **llevarse bien/mal**

llover a cántaros *exp.* to rain cats and dogs • (lit); to rain pitcherfuls.
SYNONYM (1): **llover a chorros** *exp.* • (lit); to rain in spurts.
SYNONYM (2): **llover con rabia** *exp.* (Cuba, Puerto Rico, Dominican Republic) • (lit); to rain with anger (or fury).
SYNONYM (3): **caer burros aparejados** *exp.* (Cuba, Puerto Rico, Dominican Republic) • (lit); to fall prepared donkeys.

-M-

malísimamente *adv.* very badly, terribly.
NOTE: This comes from the adverb *mal* meaning "poorly."

mandar a alguien a bañar *exp.* • to tell someone to go take a flying leap! • (lit); to send someone to go take a bath • *¡Vete a bañar!;* Go fly a kite!
NOTE: The following are other ways to say, "Go fly a kite!"
(1): **¡Vete a ver si ya puso la cochina/puerca!** *exp.* • (lit); Go see if the sow has already laid an egg.
(2): **¡Vete a echar pulgas a otra parte!** *exp.* • (lit); Go throw fleas somewhere else.
(3): **¡Vete a freír espárragos!** *exp.* (lit); Go fry asparagus.
(4): **¡Vete a freír chongos!** *exp.* (Mexico) • (lit); Go fry buns!

(5): **¡Vete a freír monos!** *exp.*
(Colombia) • (lit); Go fry
monkeys!
(6): **¡Vete a freír mocos!** *exp.*
(Ecuador, Peru, Bolivia) • (lit);
Go fry mucus!

**mandar a alguien a freír
espárragos** *exp.* to tell someone
to take a flying leap • (lit); to
send someone to fry asparagus.
SYNONYM: **mandar a alguien a
freír monas** *exp.* • (lit); to send
someone to fry female monkeys.

más de cuatro *exp.* several people •
(lit); more than four (people).

más loco(a) que un(a) chivo(a) *exp.*
(Cuba, Puerto Rico, Dominican
Republic) to be out of one's
mind, to be crazy • (lit); to be
crazier than a young goat.

más vale tarde que nunca *exp.*
better late than never • (lit); it is
worth more late than never.

matar dos pájaros de un tiro *exp.* to
kill two birds with one stone •
(lit); to kill two birds with one
throw.

media naranja *f.* better half, spouse
• (lit); **1.** half an orange • **2.**
dome, cupola.
NOTE: In Spanish, a dome is
called a *media naranja* or literally,
"half an orange" because of its
shape. *Media naranja* is
commonly used as a humorous
and affectionate term for one's
spouse since one half completes
the other as would two halves of
an orange.

SYNONYM: **mitad** *f.* • (lit); half •
mi cara mitad; my better half.

meter la cuchara *exp.* to meddle, to
butt in • (lit); to put the spoon in.

**meter las narices en lo que a uno
no le importa** *exp.* to butt into
other people's business, to poke
(to stick) one's nose into
everything • (lit); to put the nose
into that which doesn't concern
one.
ALSO: **en sus mismas narices** *exp.*
right under one's very nose •
(lit); in one's own nose.

meterse con *exp.* to pick a fight
with, to quarrel with • (lit); to
put oneself with.

meterse en buen lío *exp.* to get
oneself into a fine mess • (lit); to
put oneself in a good bundle.

**meterse entre las patas de los
caballos** *exp.* to get into trouble •
(lit); to put oneself between the
horses' feet.

mirar con el rabo del ojo *exp.* to
look out of the corner of one's
eye • (lit); to look out with the
tail of the eye • *Me miró con el
rabo del ojo;* He/She looked at me
out of the corner of his/her eye.

mirar por sus intereses *exp.* to look
out for oneself, to look out for
number one • (lit); to look out
for one's interests.
ALSO: **mirar bien/mal a uno** *exp.*
to like/dislike someone • (lit); to
look someone well/badly.

morderse la lengua *exp.* to hold or control one's tongue • (lit); to bite one's tongue.
ANTONYM (1): **no morderse la lengua** *exp.* not to mince words, to speak straight from the shoulder • (lit); not to bite one's tongue.
ANTONYM (2): **cantar claro** *exp.* • (lit); to sing clearly.
ANTONYM (3): **ser claridoso(a)** *exp.* (Venezuela, Central America) • (lit); to be very clear.

morirse de aburrimiento *exp.* to be bored to death, bored stiff • (lit); to die of boredom.
SYNONYM: **aburrirse como una ostra** *exp.* • (lit); to bore oneself like an oyster.

muy allá *exp.* miles away, much further on • (lit); very there.
NOTE: This is generally a very popular idiomatic expression.

-N-

nacer de pie *exp.* to be born lucky • (lit); to be born (on foot) standing
SYNONYM (1): **nacer parado(a)** *exp.* • (lit); to be born standing.
SYNONYM (2): **nacer con estrella** *exp.* to be born under a lucky star • (lit); to be born with star.

nacer parado(a) *exp.* to be born lucky • (lit); to be born standing.

nadar entre dos aguas *exp.* to be undecided, on the fence • (lit); to swim between two waters.
SYNONYM (1): **entre azul y buenas noches** *exp.* • (lit); between blue and good night.
SYNONYM (2): **ni un sí ni un no** *exp.* • (lit); not a yes nor a no.

narizón *adj.* big-nosed.
NOTE (1): This comes from the feminine noun *nariz* meaning "nose." In Spanish, special suffixes are commonly attached to nouns, adjectives, and adverbs to intensify their meaning. In this case, the suffix *zón* is added to the word *nariz*, transforming it into *narizón* or "honker, schnozzola, etc." In saying "Look at his big nose!" it would certainly be more colloquial to say ¡*Mira su narizón!* rather than ¡*Mira su gran nariz!* The same would apply to other nouns as well, such as *cabeza* meaning "head": ¡*Mira su cabezón!* rather than ¡*Mira su gran cabeza!*
NOTE (2): When a noun is modified using the suffix *zón*, it may be used interchangeably as an adjective.

no dar el brazo a torcer *exp.* to stick to one's guns, not to give in, not to have one's arm twisted • (lit); not to give one's arm to be twisted.
ANTONYM: **dar el brazo a torcer** *exp.* to give in, to have one's arm twisted • (lit); to give one's arm to be twisted.

no decir ni pío *exp.* not to say a word, not to say a peep • (lit); not to say a chirp.
ALSO: **pío** *m.* desire, yearning • (lit); chirping, clucking.

no dejar piedra por mover *exp.* to leave no stone unturned • (lit); not to leave a stone to be moved.

no entender ni papa *exp.* not to understand a thing • (lit); not to understand a potato.
ALSO: **no saber ni papa de** *exp.* not to know a thing about, not to have a clue about • (lit); not to know a potato about.
NOTE: **papa** *f.* potato • **papa** *m.* Pope • **papá** *m.* father, daddy.

no haber inventado la pólvora *exp.* to be no genius, to be thick-skinned • (lit); not to have invented gunpowder.
ALSO: **gastar (la) pólvora en salvas** *exp.* to waste one's efforts • (lit); to waste gunpowder in vollies.

¡no hay pero que valga! *exp.* no buts about it! • (lit); there is no but that is worthwhile.
NOTE: This expression can also be used in the plural: *¡No hay peros que valgan!*

no importar un bledo *exp.* not to give a darn about (something) • (lit); it doesn't matter one goosefoot plant.

no mover un dedo *exp.* not to lift a finger • (lit); not to move a finger.

no poder más *exp.* to be exhausted • (lit); to be unable to do anything more.
SYNONYM (1): **tener los huesos molidos** *exp.* • (lit); to have one's bones ground up (or more literally, to be tired to the bone).

SYNONYM (2): **estar molido(a)** *exp.* to be ground up or pulverized.
SYNONYM (3): **estar muerto(a)** *exp.* • (lit); to be dead (tired).
SYNONYM (4): **estar más muerto(a) que vivo(a)** *exp.* • (lit); to be more dead than alive.

no poder ver a uno ni en pintura *exp.* not to be able to stand someone • (lit); not to be able to even look at a painting of someone (as just their mere image would be too much to bear).
SYNONYM (1): **no poder con** *exp.* • (lit); not to be able to put up with.
SYNONYM (2): **no ser un hueso fácil de roer** *exp.* not to be easy to tolerate • (lit); not to be an easy bone to gnaw.
SYNONYM (3): **no tragar a alguien** *exp.* not to be able to stomach someone • (lit); not to swallow someone.

no poder ver gota *exp.* not to be able to see a thing • (lit); not to be able to see a drop.

no saber dónde meterse *exp.* not to know where to turn • (lit); not to know where to put oneself.

no saber ni jota *exp.* not to know a thing about, not to know beans about • (lit); not to know a "j" about (something).

no ser cosa de juego *exp.* to be no laughing matter • (lit); not to be a thing of game.
ALSO: **hacer doble juego** *exp.* to be two-faced • (lit); to make double game.

no tener corazón para *exp.* • (lit);
not to have a heart to (do
something).
SYNONYM: **ser blando(a) de
corazón** *exp.* to be soft-hearted •
(lit); to be soft of the heart.
ANTONYM: **tener (el) corazón de
piedra** *exp.* to be hardhearted •
(lit); to have a heart of stone.
ALSO (1): **tener corazón de pollo**
exp. to be softhearted • (lit); to
have a chicken heart.
ALSO (2): **ser de buen corazón**
exp. to be kindhearted • (lit); to
be of good heart.
ALSO (3): **no tener corazón** *exp.* to
be heartless • (lit); not to have
(a) heart.

no tener dónde caerse muerto *exp.*
to be flat broke • (lit); not to
have a place to fall down dead.

no tener nada que ver con *exp.* to
have nothing to do with • (lit);
to have nothing to see with.
SYNONYM: **no tener arte ni parte
en** *exp.* not to have art nor part
with.

no tener nombre *exp.* to be
unspeakable • (lit); not to have a
name • *Es tan absurdo que no tiene
nombre;* It's so absurd I don't
even know what to call it.

no tener pelos en la lengua *exp.* not
to mince one's words, to be
outspoken • (lit); not to have
hairs on the tongue.
ALSO: **buscar pelos en la sopa**
exp. to find fault with
everything, to nit-pick • (lit); to
look for hairs in the soap.

no ver un burro a tres pasos *exp.* to
be as blind as a bat • (lit); not to
see a donkey at three paces.
ALSO: **burro** *m.* dumb • (lit);
donkey.

nones *adv.* (Mexico) no, nope.
SYNONYM: **nel** *adv.* (Mexico)

-O-

O.K. *interj.* (Americanism) okay.
NOTE: This interjection has been
borrowed from English and is
becoming increasingly popular
throughout the
Spanish-speaking countries.
SYNONYM: **vale** *interj.* (Spain) •
¡Vale!; Okay! • (lit); worth •
NOTE: This comes from the verb
valer meaning "to be worth. •
ALSO: **¡Sí, vale!** *interj.* Why, yes!

oír decir que *exp.* to hear that • (lit);
to hear said that.
NOTE: A common mistake made
by Spanish students who are
trying to say "to hear that" is to
say *oír que* instead of *oír decir que.*
In the dialogue, the phrase, *He
oído decir que es fabulosa,* was
used, which literally translates as
"I have heard say that it's
fabulous." Although the literal
translation of *He oído que es
fabulosa* is indeed "I have heard
that it's fabulous," this would be
incorrect Spanish.
SEE: **oír hablar de** *(p. 155)*

oír hablar de *exp.* to hear of
(something) • (lit); to hear speak
of (something).

NOTE: Many students of Spanish make the common mistake of using *oír de* instead of *oír hablar de*. Although the literation translation of *oír de* is indeed "to hear of," this is not a correct Spanish expression. For example: *He oído hablar de ella;* "I've heard of her." It would *not* be correct to say: *He oído de ella.* The same holds true for the expression *oír decir que* not *oír que,* another common mistake made by Spanish students who are trying to say "to hear that." For example: *He oído decir que su mamá está enferma;* I've heard (say) that her/his mother is sick. It would *not* be correct to say: *He oído que su mamá está enferma.*

-P-

padre *adj.* (Mexico) **1.** nice, pleasant, enjoyable • **2.** huge • (lit); father.

pagar al contado *exp.* to pay cash • (lit); to pay counted.

para chuparse los dedos *exp.* delicious • (lit); to suck or lick one's fingers.
NOTE: A popular Spanish advertisement: *Kentucky Fried Chicken está para chuparse los dedos;* Kentucky Fried Chicken is finger lickin' good.

¿para qué? *conj.* why? what for? • (lit); for what?

párrafo aparte *exp.* not to change the subject but • (lit); paragraph aside.

partirle el corazón a uno *exp.* • (lit); to break someone's heart.

pasar por alto *exp.* to ignore, overlook, or pass over • (lit); to pass for tall.

pasarse de raya *exp.* to go too far, to overstep one's bounds • (lit); to cross the line.

pasta *f.* (Spain) dough, cash, loot • (lit); paste or dough.
ALSO: **tener pasta de** *exp.* to have the makings of • (lit); to have the paste of.

patinarle el coco *exp.* to be missing a screw, to be slipping • (lit); to spin one's coconut.
SYNONYM (1): **traer frito a uno** *exp.* • (lit); to bring fried to someone.
SYNONYM (2): **traer loco a uno** *exp.* • (lit); to bring craziness to someone.

pegársele como una ladilla *exp.* (somewhat vulgar, use with discretion) to stick to someone like glue • (lit); to stick to someone like a crab (as in pubic lice).
ALSO: **pegarle cuatro gritos a alguien** *exp.* to give someone a piece of one's mind, to rake someone over the coals • (lit); to let out four screams to someone.

pensar para sus adentros *exp.* to think to oneself • (lit); to think by one's insides.

perder el habla *exp.* to be speechless • (lit); to lose one's speech.
SYNONYM: **quedarse mudo** *exp.* • (lit); to remain mute.

perder los estribos *exp.* to lose control, to lose one's head, to lose one's temper • (lit); to lose the stirrups.

pez gordo *exp.* person of importance, "bigwig" • (lit); fat fish.
SYNONYM: **de peso** *exp.* • (lit); of weight, weighty • *Ese señor es una persona de peso;* That man's a bigwig.

poner a uno al día *exp.* to bring someone up-to-date • (lit); to put one at the day.
NOTE: **estar al día** *exp.* to be up-to-date.
SYNONYM (1): **poner a uno al corriente** *exp.* • (lit); to put one at the current (moment).
SYNONYM (2): **poner a uno al tanto** *exp.* • (lit); to put one at the point (in a score).

poner a uno como un trapo *exp.* to rake someone over the coals • (lit); to put one like a rag.
SYNONYM: **poner a uno como campeón** *exp.* (Mexico) • (lit); to put one like a champion.

poner al corriente *exp.* to bring up-to-date, to inform, to give the lowdown • (lit); to put in the current or "in the flow of knowledge."
SYNONYM: **poner al día** *exp.* • (lit); to put to the day.

ALSO (1): **corriente** *f.* trend • *las últimas corrientes de la moda;* the latest fashion trends.
ALSO (2): **llevarle/seguirle la corriente a uno** *exp.* to humor someone, to go right along with that which is being said • (lit); to carry/to follow the current to someone.

poner el grito en el cielo *exp.* to raise the roof, to scream with rage • (lit); to put a scream in the sky.

ponerse a flote *exp.* to get back up on one's own two feet again • (lit); to put oneself afloat.
SYNONYM: **levantar cabeza** *exp.* • (lit); to lift the head • NOTE: This could best be compared to the American expression, "to hold up one's head" or "to pull oneself back up."

ponerse rojo(a)/colorado(a) *exp.* to blush, to get red in the face • (lit); to put oneself (to become) red.
SYNONYM (1): **acholar(se)** *v.* (Ecuador, Peru) • (lit); to shame (oneself).
SYNONYM (2): **ruborizarse** *v.* (Latin America) • (lit); to make oneself blush.
ALSO (1): **poner rojo/colorado a alguien** *exp.* to make someone blush • (lit); to put someone red.
ALSO (2): **un chiste rojo** *exp.* a dirty joke • (lit); a red joke.

ponérsele a uno la carne de gallina *exp.* to get goose bumps • (lit); to have one's flesh turn into that of a hen • *Me pone la carne de* *gallina;* It gives me goose bumps. ALSO: **gallina** *m. & f.* coward, "chicken" • (lit); chicken • *Es una gallina;* He's/She's a coward.

ponérsele los pelos de punta *exp.* to have one's hair stand on end • (lit); to put one's hairs on end. ALSO: **cortar/partir un cabello en el aire** *exp.* to split hairs • (lit); to cut/to split a hair in the air.

por el estilo *exp.* of that sort • (lit); in the style • **1.** *En el fuego, perdí una televisión, un piano y cosas por el estilo;* In the fire, I lost a television, a piano, and things of that sort • **2.** *Me dijo que era profesor o algo por el estilo;* He told me he was a teacher or something like that.

por fin *exp.* at last, finally • (lit); to the end • *Al fin llegó;* At last, he/she showed up.

por lo visto *exp.* apparently, by the looks of, obviously • (lit); by what is seen. SYNONYM: **está visto que** *exp.* it's obvious that • (lit); it's seen that.

por supuesto *exp.* of course, certainly • (lit); for supposed • *¿Hiciste tu tarea? ¡Por supuesto!;* Did you do your homework? Of course!

por una parte... y por otra *exp.* on the one hand... and the other • (lit); for one part and for another. ALSO: **de parte a parte** *exp.* back and forth, from one side to the other. SYNONYM: **por un lado... y por**

otro *exp.* • (lit); for one side... and for the other.

puras mentiras *exp.* pure lies. NOTE: The adjective *puro* can be used to mean "complete" or "utter" as in the expression *puras papas* meaning "absolutely nothing": *¿Qué te dio para tu cumpleaños? -¡Puras papas!;* -What did he/she give you for your birthday? -Absolutely nothing! • *pura flojera:* pure laziness • (lit); pure looseness.

-Q-

¡Qué lata! *exp.* What a drag! What a nuisance! What a bore! • (lit); What a tin can!

¡Qué va! *exclam.* Baloney! No way! Get out of here! • (lit); What goes! SYNONYM (1): **¡Qué disparate!** *exclam.* What baloney! SYNONYM (2): **¡Qué tontería!** *exclam.* What stupidity! SYNONYM (3): **¡Qué bobada!** *exclam.* What nonsense!

¡qué... ni qué ocho cuartos! *exp.* my foot! NOTE: When this expression surrounds a noun, such as *¡Qué novias ni qué ocho cuartos!* the free translation becomes "Girl friends, my eye!" • This expression does not lend itself to a literal translation.

¿qué hay de nuevo? *exp.* • (lit); What's new?

NOTE: **de nuevo** *adv.* again • *Lo hizo de nuevo;* He/She did it again.
SYNONYM: **¿Qué hubo?** *exp.* (Mexico, Colombia) What's up?

¿qué mosca te pica? *exp.* what's eating you?

quedarle bien *exp.* to fit someone well, to be becoming (on someone) • (lit); to remain well on someone.

quitarse los años *exp.* to lie about one's age • (lit); to take off one's years.

-R-

rascarse el bolsillo *exp.* to cough up money • (lit); to scratch one's pocket.
ALSO: **rascar** *v.* to play the guitar • (lit); to scratch (away at) • **rascatripas** *m.* third-rate violin player.

ratón de biblioteca *exp.* bookworm • (lit); library mouse.

ratos libres *exp.* in spare time, in leisure hours • (lit); free moments.
SYNONYM: **a ratos perdidos** *exp.* in lost moments.

reír a carcajadas *exp.* to laugh uproariously • (lit); to laugh at guffaws.
ALSO (1): **soltar una carcajada** *exp.* to guffaw, to burst out laughing • (lit); to release a guffaw.
ALSO (2): **una buena carcajada** *exp.* a hearty laugh • (lit); a good guffaw.

reventar *v.* **1.** to annoy, to bother, to irritate • **2.** to tire someone out • (lit); to burst.

revolverle las tripas *exp.* to turn one's stomach • (lit); to stir one's guts.
SYNONYM: **revolverle el estómago** *exp.* • (lit); to stir one's stomach.

romper a *exp.* to begin to, to burst out, to suddenly start to • (lit); to break (out) to.
SYNONYM(1): **echarse a** *exp.* to begin to, to burst out, to suddenly start to • (lit); to throw oneself to • *echarse a reír/llorar;* to burst out laughing/crying.
SYNONYM(2): **deshacerse en** *v.* • (lit); to undo oneself in.

romper con *exp.* to break up with • (lit); to break with.
SYNONYM: **tronar con** *v.* to break off relations with • (lit); to thunder.

romper el hielo *exp.* • (lit); to break the ice.
ALSO: **estar hecho un hielo** *exp.* to be frozen, to be freezing cold • (lit); to have become an ice.

romperle a alguien la cara *exp.* to punch someone in the nose, to smash someone's face in • (lit); to break someone's face.
SYNONYM: **caerle a puñetazos a alguien** *exp.* • (lit); to have someone fall with punches.

romperle la crisma a alguien *exp.*
to break someone's head • (lit);
to break one's chrism.
SYNONYM (1): **romperle el
bautismo** *exp.* • (lit); to break
one's baptism.
SYNONYM (2): **romperle la cara (a
alguien)** *exp.* to smash
someone's face • (lit); to break
someone's face.
NOTE: **crisma** *f.* head • (lit);
chrism.

romperse/calentarse la cabeza *exp.*
to rack one's brains • (lit); to
break/heat up one's head.
SYNONYM: **romperse/calentarse
los cascos** *exp.* • (lit); to break/to
heat up one's skull.

-S-

sacar de quicio a uno *exp.* to
exasperate or infuriate someone
• (lit); to take someone out of a
doorjamb.
SYNONYM: **freír** *v.* • (lit); to fry.

salir a pedir de boca *exp.* to go
perfectly • (lit); to come out to
ask from the mouth.
SYNONYM: **salir al pelo** *exp.* to
work to a "T" • (lit); to come out
to the hair.

salir el tiro por la culata *exp.* to
backfire • (lit); to have the shot
go out the breech or butt (of a
firearm).

saltar a la vista *exp.* to be obvious •
(lit); to jump to the sight.

SYNONYM: **saltar a los ojos** *exp.* •
(lit); to jump to the eyes.

saltarse la tapa de los sesos *exp.* to
blow one's brains out • (lit); to
blow up the lid of the brains.
ALSO: **perder el seso** *exp.* to lose
one's head, to go out of one's
mind • (lit); to lose the brain.

sentar como anillo al dedo *exp.* to
fit like a glove • (lit); to fit like a
ring on a finger.
ALSO: **venir como anillo al dedo**
exp. to be just what the doctor
ordered, to be just what one was
hoping for • (lit); to come like a
ring to the finger.

ser blando(a) de corazón *exp.* to be
soft-hearted • (lit); to be soft of
the heart.
ALSO: **blando(a)** *adj.* easy • (lit);
soft • *Una vida blanda;* An easy
life.
ANTONYM: **tener corazón de
piedra** *exp.* to be hard-hearted •
(lit); to have a heart of stone.

ser bobo(a) *adj.* to be silly, stupid,
foolish. • (lit); to be naive,
simple.

ser buena onda *exp.* (Mexico) to be
a "good egg" • (lit); to be a good
wave.

ser de pacotilla *exp.* to be worthless
junk • (lit); to be trash.
SYNONYM (1): **no valer un comino**
exp. • (lit); not to be worth a
cumin.
SYNONYM (2): **no valer un
cacahuete** *exp.* (Mexico) • (lit);
not to be worth a peanut.
SYNONYM (3): **no valer un cacao**

exp. (Central America) • (lit); not to be worth a cocoa bean.
SYNONYM (4): **no valer un palo de tabaco** *exp.* (Colombia) • (lit); not to be worth a stick of tobacco.
SYNONYM (5): **no valer un taco** *exp.* (Colombia) • (lit); not to be worth a taco.
SYNONYM (6): **estar para el gato** *exp.* (Chile) • (lit); to be for the cat (or: something the cat dragged in).

ser duro(a) de oído *exp.* to be hard of hearing • (lit); to be hard of hearing.
SYNONYM: **ser sordo(a) como una tapia** *exp.* • (lit); to be deaf as a wall.

ser escupida de *exp.* to be the spit and image of • (lit); to be the spit of.
NOTE: *Es escupida de su madre;* (lit); She's the spit of her mother [or] *Es su madre escupida;* (lit) It's her mother spit (out).

ser la comidilla del pueblo *exp.* to be the talk of the town • (lit); to be the little food of the town.
SYNONYM: **andar en boca de todos** *exp.* everyone's talking about it • (lit); to go about in everyone's mouth.

ser la oveja negra de la familia *exp.* • (lit); to be the black sheep of the family.

ser más pobre que una rata *exp.* to be stone-broke • (lit); to be as poor as a rat.
NOTE: This could best be compared to the American

expression, "to be as poor as a church mouse."
ALSO: **rata/ratero(a)** *n.* thief.
SYNONYM: **pelado(a)** *adj.* • (lit); peeled.

ser muy ligero(a) de palabra *exp.* to be very talkative • (lit); to be very light with words.

ser otro cantar *exp.* to be another story • (lit); to be another song.
SYNONYM (1): **ser harina de otro costal** *exp.* • (lit); to be flour of a different sack • *Eso es harina de otro costal;* That's a different story.
SYNONYM: **no viene al cuento** *exp.* • (lit); it doesn't come to the story.

ser pan comido *exp.* to be easy, a cinch • (lit); to be eaten bread.

ser pesado(a) *adj.* to be boring, dull, unpleasant • (lit); to be heavy.

ser un cero a la izquierda *exp.* said of someone who is a real zero, who will never amount to anything • (lit); to be a zero to the left (of the decimal point).

ser uña y carne *exp.* to be inseparable, to be hand in glove • (lit); to be fingernail and flesh.
ALSO: **esconder las uñas** *exp.* to hide one's true intentions • (lit); to hide the fingernails •
ANTONYM: **sacar las uñas** *exp.* to show one's true colors.

sin falta *exp.* without fail • (lit); without fault.

sin faltar una coma *exp.* down to the last detail • (lit); without

missing a comma.
SYNONYM: **con puntos y comas**
exp. • (lit); with periods and
commas.

sin más ni más *exp.* just like that •
(lit); without anything further or
anything more.

sin número *exp.* countless • (lit);
without number.
ALSO: **número** *m.* performance
(of a cabaret, circus, etc.).

sobre gustos no hay nada escrito
exp. to each his own (taste) • (lit);
on tastes, there is nothing
written (meaning: when it comes
to tastes, there are no rules).
SYNONYM: **en gustos se rompen
géneros** *exp.* • (lit); in tastes,
styles are broken.

son como *exp.* used when
indicating an approximate time,
i.e. *Son como las 5:00;* It's around
5:00 • SEE: **en punto**

sonarle *v.* to sound familiar (to
one), to ring a bell (in one's
memory) • (lit); to sound to one.
ALSO: **sonarse** *v.* to blow one's
nose • (lit); to sound oneself •
NOTE: This is short for *sonarse las
narices* which literally means "to
sound the nostrils."

sudar la gota gorda *exp.* to sweat
blood, to make a superhuman
effort • (lit); to sweat the fat
drop.
ALSO (1): **sudar a chorros** *exp.* to
sweat like a pig • (lit); to sweat
in spurts, gushes, streams, etc.
SYNONYM: **sudar petróleo** *exp.* •
(lit); to sweat petroleum.

-T-

tarde o temprano *exp.* sooner or
later, eventually • (lit); late or
early.
ALSO: **más tarde o más temprano**
exp. • (lit); later or earlier.

tener...abriles *exp.* to be...years old
• (lit); to have...Aprils.

tener don de gentes *exp.* to have a
winning way (with people) •
(lit); to have a gift of people.
NOTE: **gente** *f.* parents, folks •
(lit); people • *¿Cómo está tu
gente?;* How are your folks?

tener en la punta de la lengua *exp.*
• (lit); to have on the tip of the
tongue.

tener los huesos molidos *exp.* to be
wiped-out, exhausted, ready to
collapse • (lit); to have
ground-up bones.
SYNONYM: **estar hecho un trapo**
exp. to be made a rag.

tener los nervios de punta *exp.* to
be edgy • (lit); to have one's
nerves on end.
SYNONYM: **estar hecho un
manojo de nervios** *exp.* to be a
bundle of nerves • (lit); to be
made a bundle of nerves.

tener madera para *exp.* to have
what it takes, to be cut out for
(something) • (lit); to have the
wood for something • *Tiene
madera para ser papá;* He has what
it takes to be a father.
ALSO: **tocar madera** *exp.* to knock
on wood • (lit); to touch wood.

tener mal genio *exp.* to have a bad temper • (lit); to have a bad disposition.
SYNONYM: **tener un geniazo horrible** *exp.* • (lit); to have a horrible disposition.

tener malas pulgas *exp.* to be irritable, ill-tempered • (lit); to have bad fleas.

tener pendiente *exp.* to keep someone hanging (when waiting for news, etc.) • (lit); to keep (someone) hanging.
SYNONYM: **estar pendiente de** *exp.* to be waiting for • (lit); to be hanging.

tener un disgusto *exp.* to have a falling out • (lit); to have an annoyance (or disagreement).

testarudo(a) *adj.* stubborn, headstrong.
NOTE: This comes from the feminine noun *testa* meaning "head."
SYNONYM: **cabezón** *adj.* **1.** headstrong • **2.** big-headed • NOTE: This comes from the feminine noun *cabeza* meaning "head."

tiempo de perros *exp.* lousy weather • (lit); weather of dogs.
ALSO: **vida de perro** *exp.* a hard life • (lit); a dog's life.

tomar cuerpo *m.* 1. to take shape • 2. to thicken (a sauce) • (lit); to take body.

tomar un poco de aire fresco *adj.* to get some fresh air • (lit); to take a little of the fresh air.

SYNONYM: **tomar el fresco** *exp.* • (lit); to take some fresh (air).
ALSO: **ponerse fresco** *exp.* to put on light clothing (for the summer, etc.) • (lit); to put oneself fresh.

tomarle el pelo a uno *exp.* to pull someone's leg • (lit); to take someone's hair.
SYNONYM: **hacerle guaje a uno** *exp.* (Mexico) • (lit); to make a fool of someone.

trabajar de sol a sol *exp.* to work like a dog, to work nonstop • (lit); to work from sun to sun.
SYNONYM (1): **trabajar como un mulo** *exp.* • (lit); to work like a mule.
SYNONYM (2): **trabajar como una fiera** *exp.* • (lit); to work like a wild beast.

traer por los pelos *exp.* to be farfetched • (lit); to be carried by the hairs • *Me parece un poco traído por los pelos;* I think it's a little farfetched.

tragarse el anzuelo *exp.* to swallow something hook, line, and sinker • (lit); to swallow the hook.

tropezarse con alguien *exp.* to run into someone, to bump into someone • (lit); to trip or stumble with someone.

-U-

un día de estos *exp.* one of these days • (lit); one day of these.

un no sé qué *exp.* a certain something, "je ne sais quoi" • (lit); an "I-don't-know-what."

-V-

va por cuenta de la casa *exp.* it's on the house • (lit); it goes on the account of the house.

valer la pena *exp.* to be worthwhile • (lit); to be worth the pain.

¡vaya! *interj.* **1.** (used to indicate surprise) well! how about that! • **2.** (commonly used to modify a noun) *¡Vaya equipo!*; What a team! / *¡Vaya calor!*; What heat! • **3.** (used to impact a statement) *Es buen tipo, ¡vaya!*; He's a really good guy! • (lit); go! SYNONYM: **¡vamos!** *interj.* • (lit); go! *Vamos* can also be used within a sentence to indicate that the speaker has just changed his/her mind or is making a clarification. In this case, *vamos* is translated as "well": *Es guapa... vamos, no es fea;* She's pretty... well, she's not ugly. NOTE: Both *vaya* and *vamos* are extremely popular and both come from the verb *ir* meaning "to go."

ver es creer *exp.* seeing is believing • (lit); to see is to believe. SYNONYM: **ver para creer** *exp.* • (lit); to see in order to believe.

ver las estrellas *exp.* • (lit); to see the stars. ALSO (1): **nacer con buena**

estrella *exp.* to be born under a lucky star • (lit); to be born with good star. ALSO (2): **nacer con estrella** *exp.* to be born under a lucky star • (lit); to be born with star.

verse con *exp.* to meet • (lit); to see oneself with.

viejo verde *exp.* dirty old man • (lit); a green man. NOTE: In Spanish, when the color *verde* meaning "green" is used as an adjective, it has the connotation of "dirty, lewd, or sexual." In English, the color "blue" has this distinction. SYNONYM: **viejo rabo verde** *exp.* • (lit); old green tail. ALSO: **un chiste verde** *exp.* a dirty joke • (lit); a green joke • ALSO: **un chiste rojo** *exp.* a dirty joke • NOTE: The adjective *rojo,* meaning "red," also has the connotation of "dirty, lewd, or sexual."

vivir al día *exp.* to live from hand to mouth • (lit); to live to the day. ALSO: **poner al día** *exp.* to bring up-to-date • (lit); to put to the day.

volver loco a uno *exp.* to drive someone crazy • (lit); to turn someone crazy. ALSO: **loco(a)** *adj.* wonderful yet hard to believe • *Tener una suerte loca;* To have unbelievable luck.